Success
The Choice Is Yours

Success
The Choice Is Yours

GEOFFREY PRINCE

authorHOUSE®

AuthorHouse™
1663 Liberty Drive
Bloomington, IN 47403
www.authorhouse.com
Phone: 1-800-839-8640

First published by AuthorHouse   08/08/2011

ISBN: 978-1-4567-8934-3 (sc)
ISBN: 978-1-4567-8935-0 (ebk)

Printed in the United States of America

This book is printed on acid-free paper.

Contents

Geoffrey Prince was born at the tail end of the Second World War just outside Liverpool in the village of Maghull during the early hours of the morning just after a bomb dropped in front of the house. The lone bomb was a random one; the plane was on its way home after dropping the main arsenal over the Liverpool docks. Geoffrey is probably best known for his *"Thoughts for the Day"* he's been writing for quite a few years and the work he has done helping and supporting people getting started in their own businesses, through The Liverpool Chamber of Commerce and privately as well.

He himself started from scratch a number of businesses including; Fibreglass boat-building, Industrial chemical manufacturing company, A hotel converting his 150 year old private residence into a very successful 4 Crown Hotel that's still operating very successfully today; although now sold and under new ownership.

Geoffrey spent 18 years from 1974-1992 as volunteer lifeboat man with the *Royal National Lifeboat Institutes New Brighton "Rigid Inflatable Boat"*.

Geoffrey, although diagnosed in 2007 with Chronic Myeloid Leukaemia; carries on giving business people help through his executive coaching programme over Skype and one-on-one. He writes e-books, articles and on-line masterclasses.

I would like to dedicate this book to my late father William Arthur Prince, my late mother Margaret (Margo) Prince and my brother who died in 1973 at the age of 33.

"Stop looking back at what you were and where you've come from and start looking forward to where you can go. Life does have its devious turns but with a positive-attitude; you will succeed."
Geoffrey Prince 2005

"Success" is your Choice

For several years now, I think, mainly since being diagnosed with Leukaemia in 2007 I've thought more about my past life than ever before, especially what will I do since my prognosis was for only about 5 years. *"Well that's what they told me"!* I have always been a very positive person, so despite the days or weeks that I am down, Jane my wife will attest to my saying, *"the glass is always half full"* never half-empty. Over the past few years I've been thinking about what ***"Success"*** is and what it means to so many different people, also how do you achieve it.

I passionately believe that the life I have led up to now with all its ups and downs, trials and tribulations has been good to me. I have tried to do my best for my fellow man. I spent nearly 20 years on the New Brighton Lifeboat; I've brought up a family of seven, both children and step-children with 12 grandchildren. I've tried to help them overcome life's headaches and I do hope that I will be able to carry on doing so for many years to come.

This book would not have been possible without Jane; my loving wife who has stuck firmly by my side and has encouraged me so much in putting this book together. The help of a business colleague Vona Oybibo <u>vona@ sixdegreesofvisibility.com</u> who has for the past twelve months been a constant support to me over Skype, Phil Hall one of my old business partners who at times has been a pain in the rear-end but has always been there for me. John Murphy a close friend and business owner who has been through each of the chapters and given generous advice. Sarah my daughter; who has gone through the book with her business head on and again like John has been helpful in that very daughterly way. Karen another one of my daughters who suffered trying to get just the right photograph of me that she felt would be good enough. www.justaskphotography.co.uk

This book sets out to unravel some of the so-called secrets and the mystery to success and to help you define just what success means to you.

Chapter 1

The Great Mystery

"There is a great mystery or seems to be by some people that to be successful you have to be rich and powerful; utter-nonsense! I want to lay bare the thinking behind great achievement and try to expose some of those mysteries that most successful people have. I'm going to talk about those mysteries and in a few cases people that I have met and also known in my life. In some cases these people have not started out with the best of everything".

What do I mean? "The best of everything"

A lot of them had no basic education, some of them leaving school before or at the age of 15 with no qualifications, *as I did.* Some of them took a long time before they achieved success *but hey, "Success" at what?*

The definition of *"Success"* in the Oxford English Dictionary is:—

> ➤ The achievement of an aim or purpose
> ➤ The gaining of fame
> ➤ The gaining of wealth
> ➤ The gaining of social status
> ➤ A person or thing that achieves success

This book will help to show you how to get yourself onto a path that will bring both happiness and satisfaction and give you valuable techniques to help you stay on track. It gives a few more tools for you to have in your business tool-box; it's a step by step guide to your personal success. In today's ever-changing world, success should never be left to a matter of chance; *"Your Success"* is down to *"Your choice"*. If you think that success comes very easily, then please think again.

Your *"Success"* will only come from what is inside you, from your visions and dreams; your success comes from within, that burning fire in your belly that you can turn into a raging inferno. By identifying this, from today forward, from here and now, the future that you want and desire, the security that you're after for you and your family could be there to grasp.

However, *"that is your choice and your choice alone"*. We are often told *"be glad of the lot you've got"* or *"be glad of the hand you've been dealt"*. There are hundreds of thousands; probably hundreds of millions of people on our planet who don't have a choice of their own and of course, not being able to get out of the situation they're in; *"that of course is not you!"*

Just reading this book gives you choice. Choice to do what you want, choice to read what you want, choice to express yourself in public, to express your feelings without fear of arrest and of course you do have choice of very many other things; things that we naturally take for granted.

Unfortunately, we do take it as our right to have these things, to many people expect things to be given to them on a plate; well now! Please wake up and smell the roses.

An old friend of mine, Gerry White, who unfortunately passed away in September 2008, used to say; "being in the right place at the right time and meeting the right people", is one of the keys to his success. I remember so well when he was asked could he get hold of "Ducks feet" to send to the Far East back in 1973-4. His answer was; YES, of course I can! He then started to send container loads over to Hong Kong on a very regular basis and for quite some time.

"Jerry was a long-standing chairman of Wirral Chamber of Commerce and was the co-owner of the Reddington Finance Group. His group bought a 52-acre section of the former Cammell Laird shipyard in Birkenhead from BAe for £10m in 2003, eventually selling it last year for an estimated £100m.

Reddington had been involved in controversial £2bn plans to change the use of the site from industrial to leisure, with proposals for a snow dome and luxury waterfront apartments. The group sold out to Peel Holdings in 2007. Jerry made a fortune out of selling ducks' feet to the Far East and trading in lobsters. He went on to own two factories supplying cooked meats and biscuits to Britain's major retailers, as well as owning warehousing and property interests in the Mersey dock" (Note page)

I've trawled through many earlier books on "Success" from some very well known authors while I've been researching this book. Unfortunately, I've realised that most of their writings defined "Success" as making a lot of money. They seemed to concentrate overwhelmingly on material things, as the old pantomimes used to say *"rags to riches"*.

Nowadays we who are living in the present time are enjoying a great deal more prosperity than our forefathers ever did or indeed, imagined. We are certainly working fewer hours than they did at the beginning of the 1900's. Indeed, I was working a fifty-hour week when I started my apprenticeship with "English Electric" in 1958. I feel young people have a lot more disposable income to play with than we did when I was young. There is a great deal more to entertain us, tempt us and take that disposable income from us.

Primary school is the beginning of the realisation of what *"Success"* really means to young people. It's when young innocent children are hauled out of their secure home environment with their cushioned family unit and placed into a whole new world. They are immediately told *what they are and aren't good at and* who's better than they are and why they need to change.

Schools now have a policy of integration, nurturing and self development. Preschool children advance and build on a clean sheet which they are born with. Schools manipulate the building blocks which the child has put in place themselves and create a structured environment with boundaries to continue this personal development.

Unfortunately, there is a wide generation gap which has missed this opportunity and is left with either partial or no foundation blocks or personal tools to be able to develop themselves personally.

It is said that the most formative years of a child's development are between the ages of 4 and 9 years. This is when they should be helped to say YES instead of NO to visions and dreams. It's the time when the power that signals *"Success"* is the power in their own mind.

A quote, I feel very appropriate, would be the Jesuit motto, alleged to be attributed to Francis Xavier, who was the co-founder of the Jesuit Order; *"Give me the child till he is seven and I will give you the man"*. The implication is that the best opportunity to guide a person to a lifetime of belief, devotion and *"Success"* is when they are young.

Unfortunately, when I was at school segregation was rife in teaching and this was the time sports selection started with the selection of many different team games. This is where we were told what we were good at, or not so good at. It was in this very early school environment that we started to realise we were going to be a *"Success"* or we were not going to be a *"Success"* at whatever we had to do. We should be told that we had a choice, by showing us and leading us into making positive decisions in our early life and showing us that *"the choice is theirs"*.

Children are now being guided more as to what they can achieve. They are being better educated and have better opportunities in further education and there are more places available in the university system. Unfortunately, the down side to this seems to be that the work is not available to them when they have obtained their degrees. Many graduates are starting their careers with a lot of debt hanging over them! The side-bar to this is that they are starting out very early on in their life at becoming very *"Successful"* at running up a debt, with little hope of paying it off in the near future. This is one bit of *"Success"* they could certainly do without.

Chapter 2
Self-Belief

"Self-belief as such, is something that you either have or you haven't got. It takes a lot of time and perseverance to develop the skills required to alter this position. However, I firmly believe that during your formative years growing up and starting out in work, it can be knocked out of you; by family, friends, teachers, colleagues and peers.

Equally those very same people are probably the very ones who have also helped you overcome those many adversities, trials and tribulations. They are the root problem for those of you who may feel you either have it or don't have it. This chapter is based on feelings from my youth to my now adult life."

Growing up near Liverpool just after the 2nd World War was not very easy although I was very lucky and was born into a loving family and I'm pleased to say at that time we had no financial worries. However, when I was 10 years old things changed, my father died. This left a great hole in my life as I was always with him and by his side when I could be. I had as I remember a tremendous amount of *self-belief* before he died. I was always the first doing things with him, always into some trouble and always building something; my family were always saying I was a day-dreamer, perhaps I was! When my father died I think this was when I lost my direction and my *self-belief,* my anchor was not there anymore; *by the way, at the age of ten, I didn't realise this was what was happening to me.*

At school, I was at the very best, a mediocre pupil, often near the bottom of the class. I was always frightened at having to read out aloud. I couldn't spell very well and was absolute rubbish at writing. *It wasn't until I was into my fifties that I was told I had Dyslexia,* this of course explained why I struggled at things which seemed straight forward to other people. I did excel at subjects I loved; (PE) physical education, swimming, boxing, high-jump and long-distance running. I also loved working with my hands, so metal and woodwork were a passion that I could and did explore. I suppose this was my father's lasting influence on me, he was a great engineer involved with designing the air conditioning in submarines during the First World War, working on the air conditioning in Liverpool's Mersey tunnel and one of the "Queens" cruise liners, either the RMS Queen Mary or RMS Queen Elizabeth.

I indulged my love of singing, I remember trying to learn to play the violin, Phil Williams, who was my Music teacher gently, informed me, I was rubbish and he told me I lacked concentration for it. When I left school it was with absolutely no qualifications at all. I went into serving an apprenticeship as an engineer; this was great for me and with my singing in St. John's Parish Church Knotty-Ash and being in the 66th Boys Brigade; these all helped get me back to my *self-belief.*

At this time I was introduced by the Curate of the church to mountain climbing and walking in the North Wales Mountains and the Lake District, again this reinforced my *self-belief and confidence* and though I say it myself, I did reach a good proficiency at them. I decided to take up Sub-aqua diving; again this is another sport where *self-belief* and confidence play a big part.

Later I was able to go on to help and teach others to enjoy this very rewarding and enjoyable sport. It was also fantastic for my children growing up because we were away camping at the weekends with like minded families and this helped us bond in a way that had been missing in my early life after dad died.

When I started in business it was my intention to work in a business that I loved, so my first was a Mountaineering Centre in North Wales. I ran this for several years teaching and helping a lot of deprived children build their confidence and self-belief. This I fully enjoyed and had a great time doing it; unfortunately it was only ticking over and making no money. This is when I realised I needed a job that would make money so I went as a salesman for a business-to-business debt recovery company in London. After several years I realised I could run my own, which I did and ran very successfully, again dealing solely with business-to-business. In early 1972 I bought into a boatbuilding business in Birkenhead manufacturing boats from small 8ft dinghy's and canoes up to 52 ft semi-displacement planning hulls, very exciting times. Selling this I went to work as regional manager for Arrow Chemicals and when Jim Farrow sold the company in 1979 I started manufacturing my own industrial chemicals. In

1985 I sold the company and invested the money, turning my 150 year old property overlooking the sea in New Brighton into a Four Crown hotel which I sold in the early nineties. It was at this time I started to develop my ideas in helping other people in business as well as coaching and mentoring them.

You need to have total *self-belief* in yourself, stretching out to reach your visions and dreams; when you have this commitment, you will get where you want in your life. However, wherever you end up is your own personal choice. After all, you are the product of all your visions and dreams and all that you believe you're capable of doing. I've always been a believer in the true saying *"whatever you believe, you will achieve"*. I suppose over the last 40 plus years or so, I've worked with thousands of people from all walks of life, colours and creeds, through my workshops, lectures, talks, presentations and of course personal one-on-one executive coaching and mentoring, as well as in my capacity as a business-advisor. I've met so many people like myself, who've had a bad setback or a bad-start in life and yet they've gone on to achieve great things, fantastic businesses and become great role-models to the young and up and coming generations.

I do firmly believe as a coach and mentor that your life is in your own hands and therefore, interpreting that; it's in your own mind. Your mind and your subconscious will tell you; *"the choice is always yours"*. Your life is determined by your free-will. Free-will gives you the capacity to choose how you will create your life. It also gives you the ability to be *self-determined* and be able to choose what you want to do, not only to continue the old ways of the past but to believe in your visions and dreams. Remember; by taking that first step; *It's the first step to the rest of your life.*

To create more *self-belief* in your life, you need to change your way of thinking, perhaps you need to change what you are doing NOW! I know sometimes it is very difficult to admit things are not the way you planned them and sometimes after someone has said something you don't agree with, you feel like saying; *"they don't have the right to tell me that".* I've believed for a long time now that I'm the equal to most people, I've worked tremendously hard throughout my life getting to where I am today and I'm sure you have as well, so it's not up to someone else to look down on you, where you've come from or what sort of background you've had. They may have a higher education than you have, they may have been born with more money in the family but just remember your success is built on the assets you have; using those assets to the full. Using those assets wisely as you approach every challenge has probably been learned through the school of "hard knocks". In your life so far, you've made those decisions because *"the choice was yours".*

Reinforcing your self-belief

How much time are you actually spending reinforcing your self-belief? I would say probably not very often, because you probably look on it as time consuming; time you say you haven't got to spare. It probably takes too long and it's too hard and you're not really sure why you would be doing it anyway. When I'm working with clients I'm finding that they are concentrating on the most recent past experiences to gauge *"how their doing"* in their life; however, robust self-worth is not based on the last few days, weeks or even months. It's based on your whole life's experiences as a human being stretching from your early childhood to now.

You should understand that nobody is perfect so why should you expect that you should be? The best you can expect is that you will mess up from time to time you've have to understand that it's the learning from making mistakes to the understanding that it's an important part of your development. The most important and crucial part of this is only to dwell on the mistakes for the period of time it takes to draw out those important learning points and then to move on, focusing on the here and now.

Use that learning and every bit of your know-how to make a path for you to tread, hold your shoulders back with your head held high. Never be put off by derogatory comments. I have found however, *again not realised till later in my life;* that the derogatory comments are usually jealousy. It doesn't matter, whatever you decide to do in life there will always be someone there to tell you, *you can't, you won't or that's impossible to do.* Well guess what, if that's what people feel, let them feel that way and you take pleasure in knowing that at least you're trying to get a good strong foothold on the ladder of life. You're using more *tools* in your *tool-box* than they ever will. I must urge you to embrace your *self-belief, self-confidence and self-determination* and begin to develop a life full of enthusiasm. You will need to strongly believe that you can do what you want. To gain that fulfilment you will need personal change, start by embracing a simple premise; *I am! I deserve to be! I can be! I will be! I am!*

Always believe that you have and will maintain your integrity and that you will always do what is ethically right and good to do. Whatever the experience is, it will make you stronger, wiser, and more tolerant. You should always focus on the joy of living and helping others where and when you can. Try to listen to good positive people, ignore the "negaholics" and please start learning to smile and laugh more, even at yourself. Be grateful for what you have and try to forgive other people around you realising everyone is a good person, just like you and most importantly remember; always treat people the way you would like to be treated.

Now what I would like you to do is to brainstorm some ideas and complete the statements below without analysing them.

1. One of my failings from my childhood was:

   _____
   _____
   _____
   _____
   _____

2. What would I change given the opportunity:

   _____
   _____
   _____
   _____
   _____

3.   What did I miss out on when I was growing up:

_____

_____

_____

_____

_____

4.   If I'd had a better start in life, then I'd be:

_____

_____

_____

_____

_____

Have some of the answers from this brainstorming session surprised you? The outcome should have drawn some blank answers on all of the questions meaning that you where completely satisfied with everything that happened as you were growing up.

However, don't try to be complacent over the present situation you're in; I know because in the past I have been there and unfortunately the past does have a habit of catching up on you, generally when you least expect it to.

Review this chapter

✓ *Do you remember your early childhood? Write a few lines to remind you just how much self-belief you had growing up.*

_____

_____

_____

_____

_____

_____

✓ *How did you get on in school and with the work you where given, could you cope with all the things that was going on around you and where you able to cope? Dig into your memory and write a little information on how you managed, also how much self-belief did you have at the time.*

_____

_____

_____

_____

_____

_____

✓ *What activities did you enjoy and perhaps excel at as a young person. Write a couple of lines to remind yourself of the good things that happened to you. Have you carried on doing any of those activities and how much self-belief did you take with you into adult life; through collage, university and work. Don't write a long tome about it but put down how your early life moulded where you are today.*

Chapter 3

You're never too late to Learn

"This chapter will put into perspective any underlying set-backs you may have gone through in the past by helping you get in touch with the values you used to believe in. It will help you re-evaluate what you can do now and search for what you could do in the future by realigning your "visions and dreams" and helping you to take charge of your life again".

"The difference between a successful person and others is not the lack of strength, not the lack of knowledge but, rather the lack of will."
Vincent T. Lombardi

After all the medical setbacks I have faced in my life I can honestly say that if you follow the "Key steps" within this book, with the full intention of wanting to make a *"Success"*, then you will succeed. When you look deeply, where you are now? Where do you want to be in a few years? Have the *"visions and dreams"* along with a great deal of resilience and a strong *"Pro-Active"* approach to whatever life throws at you and you will certainly gain *"Success"*.

Sometimes to start being a *"Success"* especially after having gone through any sort of set-back, means the first thing you need to do is to get back in touch with your own values. All those values that you've had in the past, values that you know you can believe in. You need to start setting yourself meaningful goals again, you need to start recapping and identifying those misplaced *"visions and dreams"*; that you had and perhaps forgotten, or perhaps because of setbacks you've had. Maybe thoughts that you would never want to start again and possibly lost focus for. You need to look deeply at your own self-belief and confidence, perhaps it has been knocked about a bit, I can show you how to get from that position to where you want to be; *because I've done it!*

You need to stop looking back at yesterday, last week, last month and last year; they're gone, forgotten, you'll never get them back. Think only of today and the future; look at what motivated you in the past, then work very hard on getting it back and turning it into *"Success* "again. You should then start setting meaningful and realistic goals; goals that can be reached and are attainable, not pie-in-the-sky ones.

Now as you are gaining or perhaps regaining your self-belief and are now starting to take a more pro-active and positive approach, you're beginning to look to the future once again. You're not constantly looking over your shoulder, looking back at the past, you're now pro-actively doing what you need to do to start securing your future again.

This was the position I was placed in, in January 2009 I was forced by my medical condition to re-look at my working practice and the values that had led me to my current enthusiasm for passing on my own experiences to as many people as possible. *"Success"* is doing what needs to be done, re-evaluating what you can do now and searching for where you want to go to next, whether your goal is changing your lifestyle, starting a new business or project, working on a new product or starting a new research & development programme.*"Success"* is reached by taking control of yourself or the situation, in other words, controlling where life is taking you. This means being more *"pro-active"* in what you're doing. You will need to deal more effectively with *"stress"*, have the ability to solve problems by finding *"solutions"*. Start handling change in a very positive manner and developing a healthy optimistic outlook on life, e.g. *"The glass is always half-full never half-empty"*

Quote from Nicholson McBride Resilience quotation questionnaire:

> *"Resilience, the ability to bounce back from whatever life throws at you, is a core attribute of most people who succeed in their lives. We are interested in where "resilience" comes from and how it can be increased.*

This link http://www.testyourrq.com/ on the Nicholson McBride website gives you the opportunity, by answering some simple questions, to measure how resilient you are and receive your own Resilience Quotient score. Whether you score high or low, we hope at Nicholson McBride you find taking the questionnaire a useful chance to reflect on your current behaviour and outlook and to receive some preliminary tips on how to increase your resilience even further".

Before we go any further, let's get a rough idea of how resilient you are.

Below is an abbreviated version of the *Nicholson McBride "Resilience Questionnaire (NMRQ),* developed with the help of several hundred of *Nicholson McBride* clients and contacts. For each question, score yourself between *1 and 5, where 1 = you strongly disagree and 5 = you strongly agree.* Be honest—after all, it is to your benefit to realise where YOU really are!

Understanding the specific areas in which you lack resilience will enable you to get the most out of our *"10 Point Booster-Plan".* There is a separate column for either your spouse/partner or close friend or a co-worker to give their appraisal. This I have found is a tremendous help and support, because they should do it WITHOUT knowing what you have scored yourself.

Getting your spouse to fill in the questionnaire without any prompting from you whatsoever, the same as a colleague of close friend *(certainly someone who knows you very well)* then filling it in yourself perhaps doing an average will then let you know just what your *Resilience Quotation* is then of course you can work on improving it. Other people look on you in a different light to what you do yourself, so whatever the score is it is the starting point to changing your attitude toward your success.

Resilience questionnaire		Spouse	Friend /Colleague	You
1	In a difficult spot, I turn at once to what can be done to put things right.			
2	I influence where I can, rather than worrying about what I can't influence.			
3	I don't take criticism personally			
4	Most of the time I manage to keep things in perspective.			
5	I am calm in a crisis.			
6	I'm good at finding solutions to problems.			
7	I wouldn't describe myself as an anxious person.			
8	I don't tend to avoid conflict.			
9	I try to control events, rather than being a victim of circumstances			
10	I feel confident and secure in the position I'm in.			
Total				

0-35	36-40	41-45	46-50
A developing level of resilience. Your score indicates that, although you may not always feel at the mercy of events, you would in fact benefit significantly from developing aspects of your behaviour.	An established level of resilience. Your score indicates that you may occasionally have tough days when you can't quite make things go your way but you rarely feel ready to give up.	A strong level of resilience. You're above average score indicates that you are pretty good at rolling with the punches and you have an impressive track record of turning setbacks into opportunities.	An exceptional level of resilience. Your score indicates that you are very resilient most of the time and rarely fail to bounce back, whatever life throws at you. You believe in making your own luck.

(To go into more depth about the specific areas in which you score high, average and low, log on to www.testyourrq. com, where you will find further information about the NMRQ.)

Let me give you my example

To me, a career in sales and business has always given me a phenomenal buzz; it has its own motivation, in many ways. I've always loved making sales and the work involved in the building of a sales presentation; from the prospecting, through the presentation to the closing of the sale. Then of course following through with the after sales service to make sure you have that client/customer for a long time into the future.

Business and sales; go hand-in-glove. Making a sale, moving into a new job, starting a business or indeed any form of customer contact is SALES, one way or another. It's a genuine stimulus and it really gets your mind working on all sorts of issues. I found that I very rarely took time off if I could help it; I have to admit it was a sort of joke in the family, that even when I was on holiday I would be looking at sales, business opportunities and sales techniques as they were presented to me. As Business and sales was all I really knew, I always found it a tremendous challenge to me, it was in itself all the motivation I really needed being in business for myself. There are not many people who have risen to the top in business and the sales world as I did. Add my love for the work and the challenges it gave me, there's nothing else I'd have really wanted to do; my children would say I was a workaholic.

That's me, opening my heart, a real person a business man talking from the heart, the kind that does succeed at the very top level. It's not been a job to me, it's been a love, a personal ambition that I was able to realise and be totally happy doing it. That is what is meant by having total self-belief, confidence and motivation in everything you're doing. That's "Success". None of the above would have been accomplished without listening to my mentors and more experienced people I knew in business as I developed and climbed the ladder.

So nothing prepared me for Saturday 16th October 2004 at 1:40pm when Jane my wife had just brought me a sandwich for my lunch; I was watching the golf from Wentworth when all of a sudden I had a tight feeling in my chest; I knew something was wrong. The previous week I had been to see Sue Kidd, my Doctor, who prescribed a GTN spray and had arranged for me to go to the hospital for a treadmill test on the following Monday. I used the spray once, then twice, then Jane just dialled 999 and within 5 minutes a paramedic was with me, within the hour I was in hospital, within a few hours they had diagnosed a massive heart attack and admitted me into the intensive care unit.

Having been in business for nearly forty-five years; yes with all the up's and downs you get running your own businesses; what was I going to do? I was never ill; I had meetings, lectures and workshops to run. All that was said to me was, to think about myself only and think about getting better, not about what needed to be done over the weeks ahead. Four weeks later and still in Arrowe Park Hospital I was transferred over to the famous Broadgreen Hospital Cardiology Department. Within 24 hours I was operated on for a Quadruple Heart By-Pass and was informed that I would have to take life easier, my thought was; "Career Change"! My business partners Phil and Colin were very understanding.

So, as I always loved helping people getting businesses started and helping people keep their businesses running I was faced with being unable to stand for long periods talking (some may say at last, he may shut-up). As a business advisor I was able to take life at a slightly slower pace, choosing the amount of time I could spend out and about. I ran the business start-up courses for the Liverpool Chamber of commerce from 2005 through to 2008. Unfortunately, back in October 2007 I was diagnosed with (CML) Chronic Myeloid Leukaemia. This was when I really did have to start taking things definitely more slowly. I decided that I should be able to do more of my work via the Internet, which would mean I could work from my study and not tire myself too much.

Retirement to me was an anathema. Therefore, In 2009 I started writing my first Web-Blog dispensing information based on 40 plus years of my business and sales life. If anybody would have said to me that by November 2010, I would have developed a following and been receiving many thousands of visits on the site monthly as well as gathering thousands of followers on Facebook, Twitter and Linkedin coming from all over the world monthly and increasing daily; I just would not have believed them. Again "Success" in what I'm doing and doing it with a very pro-active approach.

Because, yet again "the choice was mine"

I have found that the social media available to everyone, if mastered is a most powerful tool in your business toolbox enabling someone with little or no knowledge to utilise it to their advantage. It is so empowering. I am saying that it doesn't matter what life or business has thrown up, being very resilient and having that burning desire to ALWAYS succeed "It's never too late to learn", is the most important piece of advice I can give.

I am now doing a radio programmes and motivational speaking engagements monthly. I'm working with John Haynes of the "International Coaching Academy" and we're running quarterly live road shows during 2011; concentrating on "self-belief and confidence building"

This, my second book "Success the choice is yours" which has kept me busy for most of 2011. I am carrying on my popular on-line presentation skills workshops every month and have started my Master-Groups, this again is keeping me busy; yet, not harassed or stressed.

My first book was an e-book "5 Keys to selling" written in 2009 and to be re-written and will be published mid to late 2012 for general sale. I have developed using Skype and my WebLog; inter active coaching and training. I would say to those of you, who are reading this book; you must embed into your subconscious; that the choice is always yours.

With a prognosis in 2007 for my Leukaemia being maybe five years, I decided to still enjoy what I love best; that is helping people and by keeping very active. This would help keep me alive and I must say that although I get tired I feel absolutely fantastic.

So in May 2009 I decided that I would teach myself; how to put together a WebLog for myself this was www. geoffreyprince.com this was to reach places around the world through the social media. It is another thing that I used to pay people to do for me; now I am able to do it myself and thoroughly enjoy the learning curve each and every day. I wake up each and every morning with positive thoughts, these thoughts in some cases I had probably written the night before and posted on my Web-Log for the world to see and, I hope get encouragement from. I must say from all the mentions I get daily people certainly seem to get some benefit from what I'm saying.

So would you agree? You are never too late to learn!

Review this chapter

Are you still prepared to keep on delving into options that are open to you and carry on working learning new skills to help develop yourself more?

✓ *Write your intentions down now:*

_____
_____
_____
_____
_____
_____
_____

✓ *You need to stop looking back at yesterday, its past; the sun will always come up in the morning it's the most basic thing. Wake up with positive thoughts not negative ones.*

Write two positive thoughts to wake up to:

_____
_____
_____
_____
_____
_____
_____

✓ *Look at re-evaluating what you can do now and search where you want to go to next.*

Write down one alteration you would like to complete NOW:

_____

_____

_____

_____

_____

_____

_____

✓ *What is your next step forward?*

_____

_____

_____

_____

_____

_____

_____

✓ *Try working towards what you want to achieve, which usually means being more "pro-active" in what you're doing now.*

Write down one pro-active thing you can do NOW:

_____

_____

_____

_____

_____

_____

_____

✓ *Give yourself thinking time.*

Write down one area that you would like to pursue further:

_____

_____

_____

_____

_____

_____

_____

Chapter 4

Your core-values

"This chapter will help you look more deeply into making correct decisions by looking at the values you hold dear, by getting you to go back to square one. Remove some of the clutter that has clogged up your thinking; which may have impaired good decision making in the past. It will bring to the front those values that have been grounded in you. Those values you've established in yourself over the years and inherited from your parents, teachers and peers. They are the values that define your character. They are the "the main tools you have in your tool-box" that you can work with. The chapter will help you clarify and identify new values".

What are your core-values? Are they your family? Is it your business? Is it freedom? Or could it be the environment? The mentors and peers you looked up to growing up, as well as the culture that you've been brought up in? These have all moulded the personal core-values that you believe in. Are you aware of your true core-values? Do you actively protect and support your core-values? Unfortunately in today's fast moving society, with so many distractions it's very easy to forget our own true values it's so easy to waste time disappearing in the wrong direction. One very important thing I say to my mentees and clients is, "take some time to think and, more importantly feel, what really matters to you". Am I still treading the path that I mapped out all those years ago?

Your personal criteria for success could be making a career or life changing decision, it's important to define your own personal criteria for your "success". Your criteria should be clearly established in your mind. You need to regularly update them because of changing circumstances and lessons learnt from the last time they were reviewed. What happens is, by making quick decisions those quick decisions could possibly send you off in a completely wrong direction. Sometimes in a direction you really didn't want to go in. I've found going back to square one often clears the mind of the clutter that we've accumulated without realising it. You need to start trying to identify the choices that you have, look at your core-values. To do this you need to ask yourself some very searching questions and being completely honest with yourself. Kidding yourself and putting things down that are untrue will not help you make the correct decisions.

Your core-values have been moulded over the years and when you're in business you bring your deeply held core-values and beliefs into that business. They mingle with the values of others within the business or organisation; this in turn helps create a better working environment. The following are a few examples of core-values. I suggest you should use them as a starting point for thinking about and pondering your values as a human being. Your core-values are your traits and qualities that you consider worthwhile. They represent your highest priorities and deeply held beliefs and your driving forces.

Some general core-values:

Ambition, competency, individuality, equality, integrity, service, responsibility, respect, dedication, diversity, improvement, enjoyment-fun, loyalty, credibility, honesty, innovativeness, teamwork, excellence, accountability, empowerment, quality, efficiency, dignity, collaboration, stewardship, empathy, accomplishment, courage, wisdom, independence, security, challenge, influence, learning, compassion, friendliness, discipline, order, generosity, persistency, dependability, flexibility and finally delegation.

(Senator John Kerry (American Senator 1943)

> **"Values are not just words, values are what we live by. They're about the causes that we champion and the people we fight!"**

Your values are after all your convictions they are your personal values and they are very important to you and cherished by you. They're not something you want or would have; they are something you literally need in your life to be true to yourself. A core-value is a principle it's something of quality that's intrinsically valuable or desirable to you. Values are very personal, they are your convictions, your beliefs, your visions and dreams, your ethics, all of them being rolled into one. When you are searching and striving towards the "Success" that you desire.

Why is it important to identify and establish personal values? It's because the values you have developed are from everything that has happened to you in your life including;

influences from your parents, family around you, religious beliefs, affiliations with any groups you belong to, your friends, peers, your education, your reading materials and a great deal more. Effective and resilient people recognise these environmental influences and therefore develop and identify clear, concise and meaningful values, beliefs and priorities. Once you've defined your own values, they will start to impact on every part and aspect of your life, which in time will have a tremendous impact on you striving towards your ultimate "Success".

Every day you demonstrate in your decision making the use of your core-values to make decisions when you're prioritising your work, at home, play and at work. In fact all your visions and dreams are all grounded in those very values. Choose the values that you believe in that best define your character. Live by them visibly every day at work, home and play. Your values are one of the most powerful and valuable tools you have in your tool-box. Your values are available for you to help be the person you want to be and to help you accomplish your visions and dreams. They will help you to reach, lead and influence others in your search for "success".

The choice is yours, don't waste the best opportunity you've been given. Because of the importance of your values I would suggest that you should *"print them out and stick them on the fridge or anywhere obvious as a reminder to you"*. [Make them available and obvious]

Clarifying your personal core-values, will mean spending time consciously developing and expanding your values, you will find it is both a fulfilling, rewarding and meaningful exercise. To be clear about your personal goals and codes of values I've listed a few below for you to draw on to expand that thinking.

> *Having a value based life is very meaningful*
> *Your life's purpose is clearer when you've based it*
> *on your own values*
> *Your visions and dreams will be very much more*
> *understandable*
>
> *Decision making will be much simpler as you go*
> *through life*
> *Choices that have to be made will be much clearer*
> *Certainly your stress levels will come down*

When you're trying to come up with a list of values, at first on the face of it may seem to be very simple. When you first look at them I assure you it takes a great deal of thought and reflection. To build a set of personal and unique list of core-values that is personally important to you and of value to you to attain a successful, happy and fulfilling life it is very challenging.

To help you identify your unique values you need to start writing a list. Firstly, what are the things that are important to you *NOW*? I have put down some ideas that will, make you think where you are at present. This is not a recrimination of what you have been doing so far in your life. It is trying to make you think of what you were like in your earlier life and where you are trying to get to in the future.

What are they?

Freedom, Happiness, Self-respect, Money, Power
A comfortable living, a loving relationship, Wisdom,
Controlling others, Success at any cost,
Write your list below:

_____

_____

_____

_____

_____

_____

_____

_____

_____

_____

_____

You should also look at:-

Who is important to me? What is important to me?
What do I need to do to feel good about myself? Am I
always honest with myself?
Am I always honest with my family? Is my family
happy with me?
Write your list below:

_____

_____

_____

_____

_____

_____

_____

_____

_____

Your first list will probably be long; which is very understandable because you are now extending your thinking and thinking somewhat outside the box. After you've made your first list, you'll start to narrow it down. This will take some time to complete because you really need to think through each and every one of the values you've written down. Remember, you'll be reflecting very hard to understand why you indentified each one of them in the first place.

When you've made the list you will now start asking yourself; what is it about this particular core-value that causes me to believe it's one of my important ones? You will now need to go through each one until you have short-listed about eight that clearly describe what you really need for your life to be meaningful and fulfilling.

What in my life **_NOW_** is important to me and therefore to my future? Look hard at the list you've made and answer these few questions:

- How do I value the above list?
- How do I stay true to these values?
- How will these values affect my life now?
- How are the values affecting shaping my future at this moment in time?

Remember; the "choice is always yours"; no one else's.

Finally choose values that are the most important to you. Look at the values that best define your character then live them every day, at work, at home and at play. Living your values is one of the most valuable tools available in your tool-box. By helping you to be what you want to be and to accomplish your visions and dreams and helping influence others.

Review this chapter

✓ *Look deep into what you feel are your values and expand where necessary.*

_____

_____

_____

_____

_____

_____

✓ *You need regularly to update your values because of the changing circumstance and lessons learned.*

_____

_____

_____

_____

_____

_____

✓ *You should use examples I have given as a starting point and ponder those values and draw your own up.*

_____

_____

_____

_____

_____

_____

✓ *Your core-values are very personal to you. They are your convictions, your beliefs, your visions and dreams, your ethics, all rolled into one, when you are searching and striving towards your "success".*

✓ *Living your core-values is one of the most powerful tools you have in your life tool-box. Can you add anymore tools for the box?*

✓ *I have given you some ideas that will, I hope, make you search where you are NOW and where you feel you want to be.*

✓ *What you should now do from this exercise is to look at where you now need to focus your time and efforts in starting to get in touch with yourself again.*

_____

_____

_____

_____

✓ *If you are struggling with these core values or how you can answer some of these questions then why not e-mail ME and see if there are ways I can help. geoffrey@geoffreyprince.com*

Chapter 5

What motivates you?

"This chapter gives you support and guidance into using the positives over the negatives. When you are making decisions that are of paramount importance in your life it will make you realise that whatever people say to you the final decision has got to be with you. Motivation is after all only a word; although the meaning to most people signals the desire to win. The desires to learn and succeed are equally important. This chapter will show you where your motivation comes from and that is in only one place, it's the fire in your belly that builds up to a mighty furnace and it's in the sayings; **I can, I will, I shall***"*.

What really motivates you? No it isn't a blue sky question; it's about what you think about the situation you're in *NOW*. It's about the driving force that produces achievements and ultimately "success". It's really a very personal thing. Unfortunately motivational coaches/instructors only try to unlock the motivation, not helping the people, by actually motivating them. It's a myth that motivation is some sort of trick.

I've found when people are placed in situations that are difficult and sometimes seem impossible for them to get out of, it's extremely difficult to motivate them if they really don't want to be. People need to have the passion and desire to have to want to be motivated in the first place. They want and need to get out of the situation there in.

Motivation is really all about your own pro-active attitude and personal commitments to your visions and dreams. People themselves need to have a tremendous amount of drive and the *will-to-want to succeed.* This only comes from within you. You alone build it through your visions and dreams; you alone can fire it up. In other words; *the choice is always yours.*

Ask any person who is successful in whatever they're doing, what motivates them? What *tools* do they have in their *tool-box?* They very likely will answer you with *"Goals"-"Self-belief" and "Targets".* Goal Setting is extremely important in motivation and "Success".

- *So what motivates you?*
- *Why are you doing what you're doing?*

If you're doing what you're doing now; perhaps it's because that's what your parents wanted you to do, or it may be through the peer-pressure that's been placed on you. You could very well find it very difficult to motivate yourself. Sure, it's possible to succeed with someone else providing the motivation for you. e.g. *"If you graduate, I'll give you a car!" or worse,* or *"*If you don't graduate, you won't get a car".

All motivation that comes from within you, you really make a great deal of difference, that's because that kind of motivation is solely driven and fired by YOU, through your "self-belief". Certainly you need some intelligence, a knowledge base, study skills, and time management skills as well but if you haven't got motivation deep within you, you certainly won't get very far.

Think about this analogy *y*ou have a car with a full fuel tank; it has a well-tuned engine and a brand new set of tyres. It's fitted with the latest sound system and the outside has been polished and looks absolutely fantastic. However, it just sits on your drive way waiting to be driven. The car has incredible potential. There's just one problem, until you sit behind the wheel, puts the key in the ignition, and start the car, you car will not move anywhere. Yes you've guessed it; the *KEY is MOTIVATION and again, the choice is yours.*

Having an interest and passion in whatever you want to do is a very important motivator and for anyone that is going through any sort of learning curve; loving what you're doing is an intrinsic part of it. The desire to learn as much as you can about what you want to do is very important. When you link the two things together you are certainly on your way to creating success. Very often *"Success"* will generally lead to more interest, which in turn leads to a greater desire to learn usually through *Continuous Personal Development*, which in turn leads to creating an upward spiral of motivation. This drives you forward toward, those visions and dreams you're after and of course the goals you've lain down and now have established.

Some people are motivated to become scientists, doctors, fireman, policemen and many other demanding jobs. They work in very demanding and sometimes extremely tough environments where the working conditions can be appalling. Customer service is a typical role where the pressures are enormous. Hundreds, if not thousands of people, provide a constant and often stressful demand on the individuals in this type of work. Problem solving, dealing with difficult customers assessing dangerous situations is extremely hard work.

Motivation and constant support needs to be provided at all times as well as *Continuous Personal Development*. This should always be treated as a priority and essential, because without a support network there will be many people who will never be able to or indeed can't handle the work at all. Your own motivation is your own fire that's inside you. It's your self-belief it's the drive you have, it's your own personal energy source. It produces the internal incentives, the ambitions, the desires and your goals and in many cases the ethics that you hold dear to you and of course, the work you do.

Let's take a look at what's your real motivation?

Are you looking for rewards?
Do you have a personal challenge?
Is it your personal desire to help people?
Do you love the work you're doing?
Do you have dreams of things you can do?
Do you feel you want to run your own business?
Is it an ambition, something in particular you want
to achieve?

List below what really motivates you

_____
_____
_____
_____
_____
_____
_____
_____
_____
_____
_____
_____
_____

Everyone has a special motivation and yours is the one
that will get *YOU* performing at your absolute best. It's
the drive that has you doing things, things that you may
not even have thought possible or indeed capable of
doing and very often comes right out of the blue. When
you're not motivated, you'll find it very difficult to get
moving. I've known people who can't get out of bed in
the mornings; you may lack energy and enthusiasm and
the will to want to do something. It could be that you're
not stimulated enough in the things or the work you're

doing, you're maybe not stretching yourself enough or; you're just plain bored with what you're doing.

What you really need is to get your motivation and your career/business balance and working in perfect harmony. They say that tomorrow never comes, it's always today, well it always does come. This is a very true and accurate statement in the context of being correct.

Before my retirement in 2009, I was organising and running business start-up courses for the "Liverpool Chamber of Commerce" and now I act as a executive coach, mentor, motivational speaker and business adviser. I can openly say I've been quite appalled, as well as thrilled, with some of the people I've interviewed, run through induction courses and helped set up and trying to guide them in business. Commitment and resilience generally go hand-in-hand; you could use the word *"stickability"* certainly you need consistency and reliability.

I have found that most people that I've helped and certainly those involved with business start-up's are people who do really want to "succeed". They are people who really want to impress on their peers and family that they are very capable and good at what they're doing, however, very often they are afraid, afraid to take the next step. Fear is good, fear of the unknown and of not succeeding means you're prepared to listen to other people's points of view. As business people, especially those working on their own they very often have no one to turn to or bounce ideas and problems off. They don't want to worry their wives/husbands or partners. They don't want to talk to their friends or any business colleagues for fear of them thinking there are insurmountable problems when all they want to do is talk things through. I've found that fear is very common.

Fear of what

Being rejected? Thinking, what if I am wrong?
Failure when attempting to do something new?
Changing what they have been doing for years?
Not succeeding, when they have made a decision?
Coming out of their Comfort Zone?

Write down any fears you may have!

_____

_____

_____

_____

_____

_____

_____

_____

_____

_____

_____

If motivation is a mystery. Why does one salesperson see his first prospect at seven in the morning and another salesperson is just getting out of bed at eleven? I don't know. It's part of the mysteries of life.
Jim Rohn

Do you know what you're really passionate about?

Spend some time in reflecting. I have found that there are many ways to get people to look very closely at themselves. One way is to have a capability statement drawn. A *"Capability Statement"* is, quite simply, a list of what you're capable of doing *NOW*. Many times over people who feel that because they have been doing the same thing for most of their lives, doing it, *day in day out,* that's all they feel they're capable of doing *Absolute rubbish,* everyone has got what is termed as *"Transferrable Skills"*.

Let me give you a few examples:—

Example 1:
Housewives turned connectionists!

A lady who we will call Susan (not her real name) came on one of my business start-up workshops. She was in her thirties and wanted to start her own cake making and decorating business in partnership with a friend. Neither had been in business before but both were very good at what they were able to do. One loved making cakes, all sorts of cakes and the other lady was extremely gifted in decorating them.

You must understand that even with the combination of the two ladies above, the business would not get off the ground without a few more ingredients added into the mix (excuse the pun!) They both came to me with tremendous visions and dreams, passion and love in what they did.

I am very pleased to say that their business has expanded very much indeed and they have been charged into making a few cakes for some very well known dignitaries and footballers they have also won a few awards for their work. You have got to have the vision; the dreams, the desire, self-belief and add a lot of love into what you want to do as well. This is certainly a recipe for "Success".

What have house-person got going for themselves?

1. *A house-person who has stayed at home bringing up children may feel that they have nothing to offer other than being a good house-person. Look at the budgets they have had to have work with; balancing the household accounts for maybe ten years;*
   Talent:— "Balancing the Books", making ends meet.
2. *Arranging the shopping from several shops, making sure there is enough food on the table for the main meals, as well as food for lunches, that's probably different for the children and spouse;*
   Talent:— "Ordering Skills".
3. *Making sure the children have all they require for school and getting them out in plenty of time. Making sure that they get to the out of school activities, being dropped off and picked up after the events;*
   Talent:— "Organisational Skills"
4. *When the children are ill and need looking after (especially if dad has man-flu!) Talent:— "Nursing Skills".*
5. *When their spouses boss comes for dinner or the in-laws arrive without saying they are coming;*
   Talent:— "Diplomatic Skills"

There are many other important skills that can be transferred into the business world and the public sector as well as other areas of life, they are "communicating", "planning", "man management" and "team building". When I have pointed out to house-persons their accomplishments, quite often they shrug them off, when in actual fact they should be proud of what they have done. Yes, they do have many more skills than the ones I've mentioned like:

Hobbies they have.
Activities they do to relax.
Other special talents they have.
Skills they have or had in the past.

Example 2
The engineer turned Thatcher

An engineer, having been working with the same firm for over 30 years took early retirement due to redundancies coming up. He decided that he would like to work outside instead of being cooped up in a factory. He saw an advert for an "Apprentice Thatcher" so he went after the job which had been a family firm for over 200 years being passed down through the generations. Unfortunately the last generation had no children to leave it to there was just the husband and wife left. They decided to take on the engineer as an apprentice hoping that the family name would carry on as it had for 200 years. The Thatching firm had on the books advance work for over 2 years and as most of the work was in the County of Norfolk, there would always be plenty of work. The engineer found that he fitted perfectly into this new role/career and this is a perfect example of an engineer learning a completely new skill and changing his working practices and more importantly "Succeeding" in turning his life around. Now after several years the business is still there and the engineer is totally happy in the career change he made and the firm is in good hands with plenty of work in hand.

Both the examples I've mentioned are two very different people, they are from very different working practices and from different parts of the United Kingdom. They do have one very overpowering thing in common; that is; *motivation.* They have done what they wanted to do, they had a vision of what they wanted and a determination of doing something they had never done before.

So please think about where you are now, where you would like to be in 12 months-5 years-10 years time. Start by making connections between your motivations and your career direction *NOW*; ask yourself; is change what I want? Please take it from me; you'll really have a great time working on it.

Aristotle
"He who has never learned to obey cannot be a good commander. We are what we repeatedly do. Excellence, therefore, is not a habit"

How do you start?

When you want to take *Control of your Life* again, for whatever reason, sit down quietly over a period of time, this will help you to relax and develop an open mind; your free spirit will come to the front. You will start to remember things from your past that you were very good at but unfortunately felt you never had the time to carry on.

A good way of finding out about what you feel you would like to do is by completing a SWOT analysis. This gives a good idea of what you're capable of doing NOW based on what you've done in the past. The SWOT analysis is an extremely useful tool for understanding yourself and decision-making for all sorts of situations, whether that's in your private life or in business. SWOT is an acronym for *Strengths, Weaknesses, Opportunities and Threats.*

"It was Dr Heinz Weihrich introduced the earlier version of the SWOT analysis, the "TOWS Matrix" in 1982. TOWS stands for Threat, |Opportunities, Weaknesses, Strengths SWOT is simply a rearrangement of these, reflecting the need to assess your current situation and reflect internally (i.e. your strengths and weaknesses) before you can look to the future and explore externally (opportunities and threats)".

The analysis headings provide a good framework for reviewing strategy, position and direction for you and for your company or for any propositions or any other ideas. Completing an analysis is very simple. The SWOT analysis also works well in brainstorming sessions, project planning and meetings. Use the analysis for business planning, strategic planning, competitor evaluation, marketing, business and product development and research reports.

So I would suggest at this stage you should do this exercise

Strengths	Weaknesses
List them down	List them down
Opportunities	**Threats**
You have now or could create in the future.	Stopping me doing it or could be from outside.

What you must do is to Brainstorm yourself!

I mentioned before that a SWOT analysis is very good in meetings; it's also very good when you are in thinking mode. Over the years, I've found a discipline of always write everything down in a hard backed A4 book. By committing everything to paper that comes into your head, it may be outlandish or foolish it doesn't matter. What matters is you've captured the moment and will remember to do something about it because it's written down. I've found that it's one of the best ways of stretching yourself. I would say; don't talk to anyone at this stage because what you are after is; *your thoughts committed to paper covering the things you are possibly wanting to do.*

 [NOTE: It's far better to hand write something down in your A4 book, rather than typing

it down, very simple; writing in long hand stimulates the brain better and you remember it]

The "Negaholics"!

What you don't want is somebody looking over your shoulder and jumping in on your train of thought, saying *"You can't do that" "You're not capable of doing that" "You haven't the ability to do that"*, *"Your uncle tried that and it didn't work"*. These people are the ***"negaholics"*** of this world with nothing better to do than criticise your visions and dreams, mainly because they have none of their own. In most cases they are jealous and very often frightened to come out of their own *"comfort zone"*

Over the years I've worked with a lot of people and shown them the benefits of creating a *"Capability Statement"* and also using the SWOT analysis in conjunction. Those who have sat down with me and have agreed to do a *"Capability Statement"* and SWOT analysis, have realised it's the best and by far the simplest way forward. It has made them think of things and actions from the past and they have found things out about themselves that they hadn't realised they could do, perhaps even been frightened of attempting to do.

I have seen myself with dyslexia; in the past being frightened to read in public, frightened to write notes to people because of bad spelling, overcome that fear and read the Bible to a full Church, learn to get better at spelling and write notes. I have seen it give me the self-belief and confidence to stand up in front of audiences of over 2000 people and speak with assurance and confidence to them.

I have also seen business people who've been running tremendously successful businesses, frightened to give a short talks and presentations to a group of their peers, overcome their fears and go on to speak to audiences in halls and theatres of several hundred of people.

When you have the correct mindset and also are being very *"Pro-Active"* and saying to yourself; *"I can do it"*, with determination and *"The Will to Want to Succeed"*, you will start to realise that the *"Glass is Half-full, NOT, Half-empty"*.

> ***Motivation*** is the fuel necessary to keep the human engine running.
> **Zig Ziglar**

Review this chapter

✓ *Motivation that comes from within you really makes a great deal of difference, because it is solely driven by YOU. Think of a time when motivation was driven by you?*

_____

_____

_____

_____

_____

_____

✓ *You're interested in doing what you're doing. Can you be learning more? Write down a very important thing you know you should really learn today.*

_____

_____

_____

_____

_____

_____

✓ *Have you set realistic goals for yourself and are they attainable? Please write down one 12month goal that is very important to you and is attainable.*

_____

_____

_____

_____

_____

_____

✓ *How can you develop the internal motivation that really counts? Write down what you think would develop an internal motivation.*

_____

_____

_____

_____

_____

_____

✓ *When it comes to motivation, the **KNOWING** is not as important as the **DOING**. What would your doing action be given the chance?*

_____

_____

_____

_____

_____

_____

Chapter 6
Realistic goal setting

"This chapter will help you break maybe one bad habit or it could just restructure your entire life. The act of personal goal setting is probably the most effective way to help define and achieve your visions and dreams. If you haven't a clear idea where you're going, this chapter will help you toward finding your way. Realistic goal-setting is a key step for charting your path to your unlimited success."

How many of us, when we come to the end of the day and feel that we've been working very hard; *find that we've been going round in circles?* Let me say, very often I've found that a busy day doesn't always mean that I've had a very productive day. Indeed very often I've felt that I've got nowhere at all. This usually means that, unfortunately, I've got my priorities completely out of sync. I have not been sticking to my working schedule and my working daily-plan.

I have, over the years had a personal mission; to help people achieve their "visions and dreams" faster than they could have, without my help.
gurugeoffrey

There have been many times in my business life I've been in this position and found that through pressure and outside commitments that my goals and therefore my prioritising has been in tatters! It's one of those things that, very slowly, generally over a period time will creep up on you; the worst part is you haven't noticed it coming.

Your time and your life are very precious!

I have seen over the year's people waste so much time accomplishing tasks that with some logical goal setting and planning would have only taken a fraction of the time.

What would you like?

- *Perhaps to achieve better health and fitness.*
- *Maybe gain more financial independence.*
- *Spend more time with your family.*
- *Obtain a higher position in the company you're working for.*
- *Gain a better direction in your life*
- *Be able to use your time more effectively.*

Remember goal setting is your road-map towards success. It will help you gain and maintain those personal and professional visions and dreams and of course, the goals you're setting yourself on the way. You can do this by implementing a goal-setting strategy that will help you live the life you would like for your family and for the work, you are doing.

The process of setting goals helps you decide on where you want to go in your life. By knowing precisely what you want to achieve, you'll know exactly where you have to concentrate all your efforts. You'll also very quickly spot the distractions we all have in our individual lives that unfortunately can so very easily send us off in completely different direction, perhaps one we should not be going in.

More often than not, well thought out and properly structured goals are incredibly motivating. Therefore, when my mentees and clients get themselves into the habit of setting and more importantly, achieving those goals I've found that they're starting to make greater strides in their goal setting as well as their self-belief and confidence. Of course, when self-belief and confidence builds, all sorts of things start to happen.

Goal setting is one of those things you either; do it! Or I must do it! Alternatively, I will do it tomorrow! Remember I've been there, as well as wearing the tee shirt. What I must say is that setting goals is not as daunting a task as you may think. One thing that you must do is to write your goals down, *(writing stimulates the mind)*. Always write them down; goals that are written down and reduced to paper are far easier to accomplish than the ones that are just *"pie in the sky."*

You need to limit the number of goals, identify what areas of your life you think needs most attention and then reduce them down to a manageable list. Only choose goals that you feel will bring you the most satisfaction; satisfaction that will improve the quality of your life. Make a list of future goals below and now promise yourself that you will only tackle them as and when you've achieve the goal you have chosen first as your number 1 priority.

Setting goals is one of the main tools you have in your tool-box. It is a master-skill towards you being a success. The more you set yourself goals and more importantly work towards them, the happier and certainly the more successful you will be. Do you realise that less than 8% of people over the age of 21 have written goals. More importantly figure of 8% earn a great deal more than those people who have not set any goals. So every time you achieve one of your goals your self-esteem, self-belief and pride in what you're doing increases. This is how you become a winner, you will become unstoppable at what you're doing, and in turn people will want to follow you because you're leading by example.

Visualise reaching each and every goal you're setting yourself because when you visualise it; you WILL achieve it. So start NOW and fill in the list below.

List five goals you have in mind for the future.	Date by when
1._____	_____
2._____	_____
3._____	_____
4._____	_____
5._____	_____

There is a strong relationship between successful people and successful businesses and the effect on the goal-setting process. By setting goals, specifically SMART goals *[see below]* as an individual and a business, it will engage the workforce and therefore encourage employees across the company to focus and successfully achieve their goals together.

Goal setting techniques are not a modern day theory; they have been around for a very long time. Indeed top-level athletes, sports people, entrepreneurs, business high-flyers and indeed achievers/winners in all fields and walks of life have used goal-setting techniques throughout history and continue to do so. *Why? Goal-setting works!* One of the reason it works is because it keeps a person focused on what they need to do and how to do it. What it's doing is to give you a long term vision with short-term motivation.

Goal-setting makes you more focused in developing the knowledge you need to acquire, it also helps you organise yourself and all the resources that you've available. In turn this gives you the opportunity to make the most of your time and obviously your life. Goals help focus all your plans, leaving you free to channel all your energy and efforts into positive action and on pre-determined tasks that in turn lead to the results you're after.

You need to examine your motivation and be emotionally involved in your personal number one goal if you're to make progress. Ask yourself why you want to make this change now. It could be because you're being pressured into doing it. You should ask yourself.

- How will achieving this goal to enhance my quality of life?

  _____
  _____
  _____
  _____
  _____
  _____
  _____
  _____

- How will I feel when I reached my goal?

  _____
  _____
  _____
  _____
  _____
  _____
  _____
  _____

Goals can be set on a number of different levels but first you need to create a *Big-Picture* of what you really want to do. So deciding on the large-scale goals you want to achieve is your first priority. The next thing is to break the *Big-Picture* down into smaller targets/goals. This is done by dividing the year down into 12 months then down into weeks of the months and finally down to days in the week, after all *you wouldn't try to eat a fruit cake in one big bite, would you?*

When you start breaking your planning down to the lowest common denominator, it has affectedly reduced your target/goals into those bite sized pieces that you require before being able to move on to the next phase.

What you now do in this process is to start with your lifetime goals and then work down to the things that are attainable today. You should write your goals down for the rest of this year, or the period of time you want to allot to it. A great number of people don't accomplish their goals because they're unsure of the correct way of setting their goals out. There is a *SMART* way of setting goals and there is the long way. *I say the best is the SMART way.*

The most effective way of putting together your intentions of setting your goals is to use the *SMART* goal approach. *It* will guarantee that your goals contain all the most important points that help you to maximise the goal setting process.

S.M.A.R.T. *stands for Specific, Measurable, Attainable, Realistic and Time-bound.*

Promise Yourself 90 Days

Commit yourself to working on your goal-setting for at least 90 days. It takes 90 days for the brain to establish any new habits or change bad habits, so you will need to commit to focusing on your goal-setting for at least that long. Promise to celebrate at the end of the 90 days-regardless of the results for having the stickability to work on the plan for that long.

> *Zig Ziglar wrote:*
> **"Unless you have a definite, precise and clear set of goals, you are not going to realise the maximum potential that lies within you".**

S = Specific: Do you know exactly what you're trying to accomplish? Your goals should be very well defined, clear and unambiguous.

M = Measurable: Are you able to quantify your progress and more importantly; be able to track it? You need to know when you reach your set goals. You will need to define specific criteria for measuring your progress to accomplishing each individual goal you've set, so as to know how to keep on track of the progress being made.

A = Attainable: Are your goals a challenge and yet still possible to achieve? All goals need to be achievable. The best goals always require you to stretch yourself but they should not be impossible to achieve.

R = Realistic: Are your goals realistic and within reach? Are you willing to commit to them? Almost certainly your goals will be realistic if you truly believe and have faith in them. You should also believe that they can be accomplished and are relevant to your life's purpose. Are they in line with your visions & dreams? All your goals must be consistent with other established goals and they must fit in with your immediate and long-term plans.

T = Time-bound: Have all your goals deadlines? Goals must clearly state and must be defined within a time frame which must include a starting date and a target date for finishing. If you don't have a time frame to work within, then there will be no urgency to start taking the *ACTION* required to achieving *YOUR GOALS*.

Having written them down, you now need to put them into a *time frame,* one that covers a period of, say *12 months* to start with. What you're now doing is breaking down your goals into bite-sized manageable items. What you've done, is to place a time-frame that is manageable, not *"pie in the sky",* hoping that you will reach them.

You're focusing on what your intention is. In wanting to attain those goals in your life and bringing them to reality, you are now creating your life! You are now taking control! You are now being *Pro-active.*

First let me explain the difference between a Bad example and a Good one.

A Bad example:
When you have made a statement without set parameters e.g. no figure, no time constraints and no plan of doing it?

☺ Good example:
When you state the obvious and how it will be done?

So here are a few examples of SMART goal-setting:

Bad example; *"I want to have lots of money"*

☺ **Good example;** "I want to have £10,000 disposable income and have cleared off all my debts by this time next year". To do this I will look at the amount of calls I am doing each day and add two more calls on new prospects. I will look at increasing the number of products discussed with each of my customers, this will also better my customer relations and create long term relationships and opportunities.

Bad example: *"I want to lose some weight".*

☺ **Good example:** "I want to lose 2lbs each month for the next twelve months; this means I will have lost 24lbs over the next twelve months. I will stop having red wine every night with dinner; I will reduce the amount of dinner I eat each night by using a smaller plate. I will walk briskly for twenty minutes every day and I will only eat starchy carbohydrates on three occasions each week.

Bad example: *"I want to write a book".*

☺ **Good example:** "I want to write a work book on "*Success the choice is yours*" that is at least 75 pages and plus of 30,000 words in length and get it completed by August 2011. I will write at least 4 pages every weekday until I complete the book."

As you can see setting *SMART* goals are crucial to your success. Once you have a *SMART* goal clearly defined, you need to come up with an action plan of how you are going to get there! Last but not least you need to take action towards your goals. Goals won't magically happen just because you've written them down. Even if you come up with a fantastic *SMART* goal, nothing happens if you don't act on it.

You still need to make your Smart goals happen by taking action consistently. Setting your goals leads to "Success". Yes we've said it before; *the choice is always yours.*

You need to educate yourself regarding your goal-setting, you should read books, blog posts and articles about the goals you're trying to achieve. Look for opportunities to listen to experts or people who have achieved their goals already. Fill your mind with these people's stories and advice and let the information saturate your world. If you wish to get more organised, try to become an expert on what organised people do to stay that way. If your wish is to climb Mount Everest, read about famous mountain climbers. *(Please make sure your also a competent climber)* Fill yourself with practical knowledge.

Find tangible ways to measure your progress, you should chart your progress on your computer, a wall chart, calendar or PDA and make sure you evaluate your plan weekly / monthly and of course at the end of the year. If you are a visual person, print out a chart that shows exactly how you are doing.

You should probably plan for additional goals, more than likely you will have more than one personal goal that you want to achieve. So schedule out a tentative plan for your other goals that you have, when your sketching out for your new goals to go after; do them when you've tackled and achieved your original goals. Dream about how much you will enjoy having more time or money or more serenity or a healthier body. As you sketch out your other goals, notice how some of your goals interact or cross over one another.

Resolve to succeed, if you're not experiencing a lot of progress, re-evaluate your initial planning and revise. Please don't be put off over your month's efforts if they don't reach where you want them to be. Carry on; commit yourself to another 30 days with a revised plan and look to bettering it over the next 30 days.

Review this chapter

Write down your SMART goals:

My S.M.A.R.T. Goals: **Date:** _____

Specific:

_____

_____

_____

_____

Measurable:

_____

_____

_____

_____

Attainable:

_____

_____

_____

_____

Realistic:

_____

_____

_____

_____

Time bound:

_____

_____

_____

_____

✓ *Why do you think it's necessary to do goal-setting?*

_____

_____

_____

_____

_____

_____

✓ *You have put a lot of hard work into developing your goal-setting plan. What will you do when you arrive at your destination?*

_____

_____

_____

_____

_____

_____

✓ *Given what you have now learned through this chapter, you should reflect and write down what may be possible for you to do in the future.*

_____

_____

_____

_____

_____

_____

Chapter 7

Take positive action

"Taking positive action is often feared, so let me try to allay that fear within you. Believe it or believe it not, out in the big wide world some people look on taking positive action exactly the same way as they do with change. I will try through this chapter to allay those fears and let you know that some knowledgeable people have been through those same fears as well".

One of the problems I've found is when clients say to me, *"I'm concerned that what I want to do, will not work!"* Please don't hesitate when you're trying to push yourself up the ladder when you're chasing your visions and dreams start by responding positively to situations arising around you. Grasp them with both hands stretched out ready to receive them, in other words; *it's a call to ACTION. It's* keeping your momentum moving in the right direction. It's the direction that you've been reading about in the previous chapters of this book and no doubt the action you've been taking on the learning curve you've now created.

If you're just sitting around in a *re-active* mood waiting for something to happen, for business to miraculously come in by itself or, by working on *"more important"* work rather than the **pro-active** actions needed to produce the results you desire, you're definitely wasting your time. You will get no closer to the visions and dreams you're seeking. Haven't you over the years realised you've probably wasted a lot of time waiting for things and events to happen and unfortunately these same events have never shown up and really were never likely to.

You need to act positively with your visions and dreams in order to get to where you want to be. Waiting around, being *re-active* will certainly just not do. Entrepreneurs aren't people who've waited for chances to come their way. They're the people that have *pro-actively* gone out of their way to forge themselves forward. They're the people that don't sit on the sidelines waiting for chances to come their way.

It's much better to act first and apologise later, than seek the permission first. We often wait for the feeling to be right; before we take the decisive action we know will bring us the satisfaction we are seeking. We must understand that a feeling of satisfaction will only come from being *pro-active* and working on a project through to the accomplishment of whatever goal we are trying to reach. It doesn't come from waiting around being *re-active* and procrastinating. ***"Procrastination is the thief of time."***

Take these examples from Duncan Bannatyne's book: ***Anyone can do it.***

I left Clydebank again and followed the money south through another string of welding jobs. Although I was still working for someone else, at least I had a trade that could potentially lead to something. At this point I had a renewed sense of self-belief but when I found myself in yet another muddy field, shivering under another tractor, with oil under every fingernail and in every crease of my skin, I realised my future had to lie elsewhere . . . I quit and decided I had to make some changes. I knew it was all down to me; I would be the catalyst, I was the only one who could make it happen. My instincts told me that I would know the right opportunity when I came across it . . .

Fed up with the cold, I headed as far south as I could get in the hope of picking up some bar work over the summer. When I'd worked on a farm outside Brighton, I'd spent a lot of time with holidaymakers; well, girls on holiday to be more specific and I thought I could handle the easy money and easy sex of life in a resort. So I got on a ferry to Jersey, where someone had told me my driving licence would still be valid. It was 1974 and with working in a bar meant that I had the mornings free, so I'd often start the day on the beach . . . I met Mick Doherty; a friendship which has stayed with me for the rest of my life.

Mick and I took a series of jobs; one week we'd be deck-chair attendants, the next hospital porters, lorry drivers or ice-cream vendors. There were plenty of wealthy people on the island, with million-pound mansions and boats moored in the harbour and very often there'd be a bit of work tending bar at a private party. That was the first time I caught a glimpse of the millionaires' lifestyle and I guess I must have thought a few times, "I wonder if this will be me one day". However, we'd often find ourselves between jobs and nothing to do so we'd head to the beaches or bars and find ways to entertain ourselves . . .

I survived on a tiny amount of money but never felt poor . . . Once the rent was paid, everything else was pretty cheap . . . Every job I did was cash-in-hand so I never needed a bank account and as this was Jersey there wasn't any tax to pay. I probably earned about £200 a month and spent every penny of it . . .

As it's virtually impossible for non-residents to start a business in Jersey unless they're incredibly wealthy, there was never an incentive to do anything other than part-time jobs. Over the years I worked out a few ways of making a bit of extra money and one of the easiest was renting an ice-cream van for the day and buying some stock. I found out that you could pay extra to get an exclusive pitch and if you were the only ice-cream van in sight you'd do better than if you were one of several around the main beaches. Without realising it, I was learning quite a lot about running a small business. I didn't realise I was learning at the time, or the skills I was picking up that would change my life, I just knew that if it was a festival day—Jersey has a lot of festivals—or the weather was good, I could make enough to take the rest of the month off . . .

These days people often ask me if I regret spending so much time partying when I could have been doing something more productive and I always tell them I wouldn't trade away a single day of my days in Jersey; it was fantastic—some of the best years of my life, in fact—and there's not a bum job or hangover I regret. I might have only had one pair of shoes and one pair of denims to my name most of the time but I was very happy there and I realise now that I actually learnt a lot about myself which helped me be more effective in business when I was older. Apart from picking up bits and pieces about the ice-cream trade, which would prove directly relevant to my future career, I got to know myself, learned my strengths and capabilities. I also got to like and believe in myself, and the idle notion that I might someday start a business began fermenting into quite a powerful brew. What was once a vision and dream was becoming an intention . . .

Earlier that morning, we'd picked up a paper to read over breakfast and I'd read a story about a man who'd started a business on a shoe-string and gone on to become a millionaire (I'm sure it was an article about Alan Sugar). It was a real rags-to-riches story and as I sat there looking out to sea I couldn't come up with a single good reason why I couldn't do exactly what he'd done.

Taking immediate **pro-active** steps, not out of fear or to force things to happen but because the next action you take will bring you closer to your visions and dreams. Then and only then, will you see tremendous results coming into your life and start to enjoy the fruits of your past hard labours that you've worked so hard to attain.

I have found when speaking to some of my *clients* that few opportunities knock on their doors, *just like that*. My answer to that is that you, yourself, only create those opportunities when you start knocking on other people's doors. I say that if you really desire what is behind those doors, then you will carry on knocking on them till they open. If you know what you're after, then you may have to break them down to get what you want. The major difference between using force out of power and using force out of fear is when you are in a powerful position you know what it is you're doing and doing it powerfully. It doesn't feel forced but it does feel very liberating to accomplish it.

Anyone, who has visions and dreams, that can't be achieved in the short term and they still take action unfortunately sometimes leave themselves vulnerable to "Negaholics" saying that they have *"delusions of grandeur"*. Where would we be without those *"big picture thinkers"? The Duncan Bannatyne's of this world. Remember it was* our forefathers dreaming big that created what we have today. The tendency to think and conceptualise on a much broader scale is a very human characteristic, just like being disciplined, or having a sense of humour, or having an aptitude for mathematics or writing.

Why is it that when we encounter these same people who possess these qualities in our daily lives, we deride and sometimes malign them? It's just as valid today as it's been since time immemorial, before cars and planes, or the computer age, or whatever. Some of us have always been disciplined and some; the opposite. Unfortunately the way life is today means that many of us are going through life struggling with big daily challenges on a very personal level. Some of us are more fortunate to be comfortable and are able to use our talents and aptitudes to make a positive difference, not just for ourselves, but for others.

So we must start by making a plan of action. *Realistic goal setting as* set out in my previous chapter. To me goal setting without a plan of action is like going to sea without charts and compass; you only hope you will reach your destination safely. The hard work you have already put in, thinking and doing your *SWOT analysis,* working out time-frames, will all be for nothing; if you don't start converting it into *ACTION.*

You now have written down your short, medium and long-term goals so you need to now be prioritising them into a logical and workable plan of action. You should think about a nice sponge-cake. If you try to put it into your mouth in one go it won't fit *(or shouldn't really).* Remember the exercise in chapter 4 where you broke your plan into twelve months, then weekly and finally down further into days. Well that's what you do with your cake; it's all cut up into bite-sized manageable pieces.

By just taking one step at a time and consistently doing something every day this will take you closer to those targets/goals you've set over the coming twelve months. Remember, they are only short term goals you've now set yourself. Your medium term goals will be to cover the next three to five years and again breaking it down to those bite sized chunks is the way to do it. After that you will know what you're after. It is always very important to have a good idea of where you want to be and to guide your business to reach those goals in ten years. So an idea of where you want to be should be roughly laid out and worked on all the time; it's an ongoing process that you should consistently be updated to stay on track.

Personal Responsibility

You now need to accept personal responsibility by forging ahead but also, by making sure you're staying on track with the targets and goals you've set yourself. It's certainly not up to anyone else; after all they're your targets and goals, so I'm glad to tell you, the choice is up to you, just you. You will only decide what you want to accomplish during the day, the week, the month and the year. Unfortunately life does have a way of distracting you from whatever action you've planned. Use the reminders and the resources of your *"realistic goal setting"* plans because this will keep your attention on your short-term goals. You must also keep them to the forefront, the longer term goals will look after themselves. Remember the saying *look after the pennies and the pounds will take care of themselves.*

Remember please live for and in the present also, be grateful for what you have now and embrace it. Look to the future with open arms and prioritise by *pro-actively* seeking and bettering what you have on your journey. Lastly and most importantly, don't ignore your reminders. If you fall behind, refocus your efforts, update your plan and change any deadlines. They are bound to need to be changed from time to time as things move on, so you should always be working on them and keep at it.

Being in business is so rewarding and satisfying, try not to stray too far off your business-plan and the direction you're pursuing. Through tenacity, drive and a positive action, your "Success" will certainly come your way. Remember; *"the choice is down to you and you alone".*

As you climb the mountain of life the work gets harder. Perseverance and consistency alone will not get you there. What will; is tenacity, drive and the "Will to want to Succeed"
gurugeoffrey

Review this chapter

✓ *Although positive-action and change are both feared by most people; both should be welcomed and embraced with open arms.*
   Can you write one or more positive actions you could take NOW?

_____

_____

_____

_____

_____

_____

✓ *You need to stop thinking that things will happen to you and being re-active and go out to reach for it by being pro-active; remember "procrastination is the thief of you time.*
   Write down a pro-active thing you've been putting off doing:

_____

_____

_____

_____

_____

_____

✓ *You need to start thinking BIG, that way you start to accomplish the small things on the way, when, eventually the BIG thinking will have paid off. We must be realistic and they should be achievable so please write down a BIG thought you have:*

_____

_____

_____

_____

_____

_____

✓ *We above all things should be prepared to take personal responsibility for the decisions we've made and not pass on that blame to anyone else. Write a personal decision you've made without passing the blame down the line:*

_____

_____

_____

_____

_____

_____

Chapter 8

Managing your time

"This chapter will help you develop a range of skills that you've got inside you head but probably don't use all the time because you're too busy thinking and doing other things. These skills and techniques on how to manage your time more effectively include tasks, projects, daily-planner, goals, allocating time, delegation, analysing time spent and many other helpful ideas and tips".

At home and work everyone can benefit from finding new ways to use time as efficiently as possible. Setting aside the time to analyse how you work can be an invaluable time-saver in itself, helping you to make your day less stressful and  more productive and supporting you through improving the use of your time and isolating aspects of your time management that needs to improve and how to set long and short term goals to prioritise your workload.

Time is the most valuable resource we have in our toolbox; it's a most precious commodity. Every human being on the earth has the same amount of time; even Bill Gates, Sir Alan Sugar, Oprah Winfrey, Peter Jones and of course **YOU**.

Sir David Frost has said, *"I don't like wasting money but I hate wasting time"*.

All the above have attained the heights they have and are where they are now, by an obsessive will to use their time wisely and to the full. If you think about it you are no different to everyone else on the planet. Why? One thing we all have in common is that we all have the same amount of time:—

- *60 seconds in every minute*
- *60 minutes in every hour*
- *24 hours in every day*
- *7 days in every week*

Time can't be saved or stored. It's not down to how much we have; it's down totally to the way we attempt to use it. Managing time is solely your decision and therefore is very personal to you. A survey a number of years ago by the Institute of Business Advisors concluded that company directors and sole business proprietors wasted 20% of their time at work.

May I suggest my top 10 time-wasters in order of importance were:

1. *Telephone interruptions.*
2. *E-mails bouncing in all the time.*
3. *People calling in.*
4. *Lack of planning.*
5. *Correcting things done by other people.*

6. *Poor inter departmental exchange of information.*
7. *Subordinates listening skills.*
8. *Middle management indecisive decision making.*
9. *Senior management for ever changing the goal post, costing time realigning.*
10. *Lack of authority by people when chairing meetings.*

So it's something you should be thinking about NOW. You need to be starting to manage your time more efficiently and effectively after all, managing you time will help you to remove a lot of stress that has built up during your day without realising it.

At the heart of time management is the management of your own time! It's more than just managing your time; it's managing you, in relation with the time you have available. It's all about setting you priorities by simply taking charge of your situation and your utilisation of the time that you have available. It means changing those habits and activities that cause you to waste time. Mostly it's about you being willing to experiment with different methods and ideas enabling you to find the most productive way to maximise the use of your valuable time.

Have ever noticed and wondered that there are some people that can manage to accomplish more work in one day than others can possibly manage in one week? When you think about it we all have total control of how much time we spend in producing or doing what needs to be done. I feel that it's all about the amount of time you want to waste. It could also be that some people have far greater energy levels than others or may be that one person is far more capable of managing their time more effectively than others are able to.

This of course doesn't mean that one person works harder but rather, the person who accomplishes more in less time has worked out how to work smarter. By planning their days and prioritising their time in a more organised and logical manner; this is how it is achieved.

How can you learn to effectively manage your time in order to accomplish more? Look at a few ideas below:

One of the first things you should think about doing is to set smart goals. Goals, that you can be realistically accomplished and setting time-bound limits for simple activities. There are some people who linger over things or indeed waste time; it could be that these people may have time on their hands time they need to fill. If you linger over things but you want to try to get more accomplished in the smallest amount of time, then you're going to have to learn to practice self-control and start setting time limits on your valuable time. You should do this by setting an appropriate and reasonable amount of time, by establishing priorities, giving individual tasks the time they require. Don't try and rush the job; because you could end up making mistakes. However, on the other hand try not to take too much time either; allocate a time-frame for each and every task to be done.

Delegate your work, don't try to do it all yourself. Don't overload yourself by insisting on doing everything yourself. Your family and work colleagues can make life a lot easier for you if only you would ask them for their help. When you're prepared to share with them, this will certainly help you get on with the more important tasks, tasks that you need to do yourself. If you're feeling overwhelmed and things seem to be closing in on you, then by simply asking for support and help will remove stress, tension and anxiety, making you feel less pressured. You should start to look at prioritising the work that has to be done and starting to say *NO a few more times, (in a nice way)*. By delegating some of your work, you're going to find more time in your busy schedule and you will find that you will start getting more things done.

I found that when I did start to asking for help and started to delegate work to others; it calmed me down, I didn't find things as rushed as they used to be. It also gave me a little bit more of *me-time*, which of course also meant I gave myself more *thinking-time* which was always lacking in the past, why; *because, I had to do it.* The relief of tension inside me was tremendous because it meant I could now *work-on-the-business and not-in-the-business.*

Organise yourself by trying to use your time wisely, not creating tasks or impossible situations for yourself or attempting to work ridiculously long working hours. Some organisations, working long hours is very often equated with staff working harder and are more dedicated to the organisation. Staff often feel if you leave on time, other staff may think you're not pulling your weight. In fact, working ridiculous long hours, decreases efficiency and productivity and can be counterproductive. Review all your outside obligations; examine each of them realistically as you prepare your diary over the coming week, month and year. You reward will be the ability to control your workload effectively and have more time to identify and focus on more important aspects of your work.

> *Peoples attitude toward time are complex and variable. If you want to use your time efficiently to accomplish all that you need to do at work and home, you need to be aware of your current habits and attitudes that shape the use of time; now.*

Prioritise your work by defining your priorities. Successful time-management begins with planning. I've found over the years that using daily/weekly/ monthly diaries as well as a *"to do*

book" works very well, mainly to keep focused and to stay on track. *I know I have mentioned this A4 book already in previous chapters; so that should tell you something about WHY I WRITE ONE DAILY.* I fill mine in with all the things I need to accomplish during the day and adding things carried over from yesterday that haven't been able to do or finish off. In my opinion the **"to do book"** is a most important book and it is an investment of only a small amount of money; money I feel, well. You can fill all your reminders, any personal activities, family things, priorities your phone calls and even shopping bits that your spouse doesn't want you to forget. I find it very useful in meeting, it means I don't lose bits of paper; the notes are safe in one hard-backed book; indeed I take mine with me to each and every meeting I attend.

Prioritising your tasks sometimes is not as simple as it sounds or I make it out to be. The work that needs to be completed and the work you need to delegate to others, you are the only one who can decide what order it should be done in and who does; should start with the first down to the least important item. In other words what's important *NOW* and what can go down toward the bottom of the list, then who will I delegate this or that task too; try not to let little things get in your way. You shouldn't let yourself feel obligated each and every time someone asks you to do something for them, remember *people will always ask busy people to do more.* This also will include charitable organisations, schools, maybe your church and should even include people in your family asking you to do something that you know you don't have the time for.

It's listing ALL the daily priorities that *MUST* be done *TODAY* and notes of those items that can wait. By using your *"to do book"* you're writing things on a new page every day, which gives you an instant focus on your activities. As stated earlier, my *"to do book"* goes with me on all my outside meetings including all the networking events and workshops that I attend. I should like to add, one of the hardest things to do and one that is very often put off by a lot of people; *is the one that you're most concerned about, the one thing or person that you really don't want to attend to.* Please treat this as a positive action, not as a negative one. The reason I mention this; is that by facing and the doing the call that you know is going to be difficult *FIRST,* means you're not having it playing on your sub-conscious mind all day. I've found that it drains you and when you are being drained in this way, you don't give you best during the day.

(So get the hardest call out of the way first).

Spot time wasters; avoid distractions and lack of focus. Identify areas of the misuse of your time, don't put off doing awkward or important things you have to do today; that's called procrastination, remember the saying *(procrastination is the thief of time)*. Set times to reply to your telephone call-backs, priorities them. If you think it's going to be a difficult call; you should really to do it first thing in the morning, getting it out of the way, by doing it then, it completely unclogs the mind and it's not playing on the your sub-conscious all day, because it will be done and dusted and out of the way. You also should set times during your day to look at your e-mails; possibly first thing in the morning, after lunch and last thing before you finish for the night.

You need to work out the best times with your personal assistant, secretary and switchboard, set times when you will take calls during the day, if you're busy in a meeting or you're out of the office you should redirect them to your personal assistant or secretary not to your mobile phone. Your staff needs to take responsibility when you're away from your desk. People will get used to this and delegating this simple task will make them feel good and you will feel far less stressful. Your reward will be the ability to control your workload by having more time to focus on the most important aspects of your job and again; *working-on-the-business and not-in-the-business.*

Avoid the clock watchers, they can come to your office last thing in the day and reckon because they've finished and they're ready to go you should be as well, unfortunately, generally the problem is that you're trying to make sure all you're work is completed for the day before you go home; they can be very negaholic and a nuisance and you need to let people know what the situation is.

Work smarter; that's what time management is all about. It's using your time more far more effectively, not necessarily working harder. The quality of your work is far more important than the quantity of it. Don't get overwhelmed by the current crisis or imminent deadlines that are looming up, crisis management leaves no time for routine matters. Remember, if you can't see the wood for the trees you will be plagued by the lack of concentration and focus which, if not tempered, will start you delivering quality over the quantity of the work to be done. Floundering around because of the lack of concentration will not help and also diminish the quality of the work. By religiously using the *"to do book"* will help stop those emotional blocks that can and do interfere with your eventual *"Successes"* these include boredom, daydreaming, stress, guilt, anger and frustration. Unfortunately, they all have a part to play in reducing your ability to concentrate.

Select your environment; by avoiding noisy and disruptive atmospheres when you're working, concentrating or studying. You need to start disciplining yourself to turn your ring tone on your mobile to silent mode, switch off the pop-up on your computer, telling you there's an e-mail coming in, also tell your switchboard and your number two, your personal assistance and your secretary that you need *[a period of time]* without interruption. As mentioned all ready you need to make set times to look at your messages and e-mails. I know it can be very difficult with appointments and calls coming in but you do need to set priorities for yourself and be hard with yourself, your colleagues and staff. Avoid distractions and the temptation to put to one side your carefully planned schedule in your ***"to do book"***.

Avoid work related stress; it is a frequently used word these days. Doctors and clinicians tend to blame it on a multitude of things. What does stress mean to you? You might view it positively in terms of the challenge to do something really well. It could be accurate to call it pressure, which is very satisfying and you may think makes your work worthwhile. Generally you should try to avoid stress because it can and does lead to sickness which in turn will alter all you're planning and throw it out of the window. Try to stay as physically fit as you possibly can. Yes, you should definitely schedule some quality time for exercising and don't feel guilty about doing it because you know that it will be helping your health in the long-term. *I for one at my age still do daily exercise and have always tried to keep reasonably fit. It has helped me fight off two heart attacks, a Quadruple Heart By-pass operation, Leukaemia and Diabetes.* Exercise is the best known way of reducing anxiety-producing stress. I have to go to the gym several times a week; very often Monday and Wednesday, I do this first thing in the morning.

✓ How do you start the day now?

_____

_____

_____

_____

✓ How much time would you like to spend thinking
   / me-time, on the you?

_____

_____

_____

_____

✓ Can you write down what you think are your top
   10 time-wasters in order of importance.

_____

_____

_____

_____

_____

_____

_____

_____

_____

_____

✓ Look at the daily planner below and fill in
   activities that you have to accomplish each day as

a priority first and then work out other prioritised jobs afterwards. You can easily make a copy for yourself and play around with it till you have a logical working one.

Time	Activity	Monday	Tuesday	Wednesday	Thursday	Friday
			Daily planner			
08:30	e-mails	e-mails	e-mails	e-mails	e-mails	e-mails
09:00						
09:30						
10:00						
10:30						
11:00						
11:30	Return am calls	Return am calls	Return am calls	Return am calls	Return am calls	Return am calls
12:00	Lunch	Lunch	Lunch	Lunch	Lunch	Lunch
13:00	e-mails	e-mails	e-mails	e-mails	e-mails	e-mails
13:30						
14:00						
14:30						
15:00						
15:30						
16:00						
16:30	Return am calls	Return am calls	Return am calls	Return am calls	Return am calls	Return am calls
17:00	e-mails	e-mails	e-mails	e-mails	e-mails	e-mails
17:30						

Now you are assuming full responsibility for managing your most valuable commodity, yes you're time. This will now lead to your taking further step towards being a *"Success"* and once again; *"The choice is yours".*

Chapter 9

Change

"This chapter I'm sure is going to demonstrate to you that as individuals we have to embrace and encourage change. In some ways all the previous chapters have something to do with it. So in trying to have more self-belief and confidence in ourselves and become more motivated we need to look deeply into our present situation first and say to ourselves, OK, so I'm here now, where do I go from here? How should I get out of it?"

Now you have realised and I sincerely hope decided that you are going to embrace change and go forward because, if you don't; you're going to start falling behind changing what you're really after and therefore the tasks and all the hard work you've been doing so far, could be for nothing. In business saying that; *if the business is not expanding; it's standing still.* In life we also have to move on, taking a grasp of the present situation and being prepared to fail. However, we do know we can pick ourselves up because in our new vocabulary there is now no such thing as standing still in fact; *failure, is not an option!* What we are now saying is, *"I will, I can, I am, because I'm now living each day with excitement and confidence".* I am now waking up every single day bursting with energy and affirming to myself; *I will, I can, I am, because I'm now living each day with excitement and confidence* and I'm full of enthusiasm for this fantastic day ahead; *full of new and exciting things to grasp hold of.*

Whether you're working by yourself or working for someone else, you will very often stop when you reach a place that you feel you should need to change. This is when you should start taking a grip of yourself and what you're doing, you need to dig in and be extremely *"Pro-active"* and say aloud *"Change, what changes do I need to make"?* You should start by embracing change, change is good and change means you're forward thinking!

Changing some of the ways you use words and phrases; an effective way to change your life is to change your attitude and mindset. One way I've found very useful is to remove certain *negative* words and phrases that we use completely from your vocabulary and replacing them with more *positive* ones. It will take time to remove the negative ones because of the length of time you've been using them. Also you will probably used to using them. However, once you start adding and using new positive words and phrases you will be surprised how people will notice and more importantly, start to react in a differently towards you. You will also start to look at the world around you in a completely different way. Your whole life will change without you having to physically change everything.

Look at the list of negative sayings:

- *I can't.*
- *The kids of today!*

- *The good old days!*
- *I don't want to know that now!*
- *It's going to be one of those days!*
- *The same old thing, the same old thing!*

You should realise that change is happening constantly. Every single day of your life changes are happening, no matter what, whether they're big changes or small ones. Even when you're doing the same old routine day in, day out, you'll find no two days will be the same. When you start realising this, even when you're facing what you think are insurmountable odds or problems or perhaps pain. All things are bearable because yes; your positive side will show through even more and you now recite to yourself; "The sun is still going to rise tomorrow" and yes, *good days* will be ahead of you.

> *Mary Engelbreit*
> "If you don't like something change it; if you can't change it, change the way you think about it."

By now you will have now begun to realise that you can and are very able to organise yourself more because you are now able to draw down on your new self-belief and confidence that's started to take hold inside you. You now know what has to be done and how you're going to get to the point in life where you want to be, your now reaching those visions and dreams that you're after. It doesn't matter whether it's a mundane task that you need to do or major change within the business that you're working in; putting it off won't get you anywhere. Change can be very difficult when we are forced to come to terms with it, generally it means that we have probably been cosseted in our safe environment and safe position, one that is called the *"Comfort Zone"*. The more change we need to make, the more difficult it is. No one likes to change. We've been cosseted one way or another for most of our lives, from the time we were in our mother's womb for 9 months, to the time we went to our first school, then when we went into our <u>BIG School</u>!

In different ways as we've been growing up it's all been change. In some ways all the above have something to do with it. So as we become more motivated, we should look more deeply into our present situation then say to ourselves, "Ok, so I'm here now. How should I get out of it?" We shouldn't, under any circumstances dwell on the problems we're facing. The problems already exist; we can't do anything about them. However, what we need to do is to concentrate on finding a solution that works.

Reflect for a moment; so far during your life you'll have been put into situations that you've not been happy with. Also there will have been absolutely fantastic times when you've been *"Flying with the Eagles"*.

I have listed a few of the more common feelings that clients of mine have often said to me:

- Things are sometimes holding them back.
- They often need to explore more possibilities in their life.
- They think they are in a mid-life crisis.
- Knowing what they should do but often can't generate the will to want to do it.

- They sometimes feeling stressed, resentful, embarrassed, angry and depressed and not sure which way to turn.
- They feel that they are at a crossroads in their life.
- They've messed up relationships with their children and they'd like to be a better parent.
- They feel they could be passing their problems and anxieties unfairly onto their family.
- They have been reading many personal development books, been on day workshops and weekend retreats. However, they still feel trapped, unsure and unhappy.
- There's a lack of joy and intimacy in their life.
- They have trouble forming close relationships with people.
- They have been mixing with too many losers in their life. They need to mix with more pro-active people.

Take some time to digest the list above; there is no time limit on thinking the list through many times. What I would suggest is to be in a quiet place, play some relaxing background music, close your eyes and let your mind wander back in time and really think of the things you want to do.

Now please write down the thoughts from yesteryear:

1. _____
2. _____
3. _____
4. _____
5. _____

6. _____
7. _____
8. _____
9. _____
10. _____

It would be nice now for you to write below some of those great achievements, as well as some small ones you've had in your so far. These are all very important; some could be from your school days, some when you were at college or university, some from your early working life, right up to the present day. I know trying to recall them is going to be somewhat difficult, it's the same when I ask clients to do a SWOT analysis on themselves; they all say *"I can't recall my strengths but I can tell you my weaknesses"*. However, I've always found this is one of the best and indeed a very good way of getting clients really filled with self-belief and confidence.

1. _____
_____
2. _____
_____
3. _____
_____
4. _____
_____
5. _____
_____
6. _____
_____
7. _____
_____

8. _____
   _____
9. _____
   _____
10. _____
    _____

If you have more use a separate sheet it's so important, when you start thinking the good things from the past the list becomes endless; yet it's your fantastic past your that you're looking at.

What I'm trying to do with this book is to show you that whatever or whoever you are, you can effect and develop positive change which will make you feel a million times more at ease with yourself. I've mentioned before that you need to embrace change with both arms open wide; you need to grab it, take hold of it but more importantly. You need to *RUN WITH IT*.

I mentioned earlier the *"fire in your belly"*. Well what I mean by that is, your inner belief and confidence that you have. I want you to start trusting your own abilities and judgement. By doing this simple act of trust you're making the most of what you have. You're starting to build more self-belief and confidence and guess what; you're starting to show people around you, that you are indeed a winner and you will be a success. I have made some very bad judgement calls and business decisions but I've always been able to make a come-back, *HOW?* I've always trusted in my own judgement. By making the most of what God gave me and very importantly getting the balance in equilibrium in all areas of my life.

One of the exercises I try to promote with my clients is to get them to look at the *"Wheel of Life"*. Each segment of the wheel represents parts of the person's life:

"The Wheel of Life" is broken into a pie with 8 segments

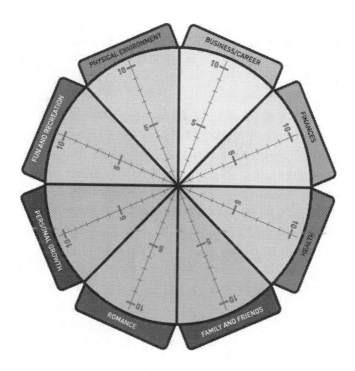

Diagram.1.

1. Business/career
2. Finance
3. Health
4. Family and friends
5. Romance

6.   Personal growth
7.   Fun and recreation
8.   Physical environment

You should plot a chart [see diagram.1.] and in [Diagram.2.] give box/segment a ranking of 1-10 (1 being poor to 10 being *"It can't get any better").*

Then you can see how balanced or imbalanced you are. The wheel of life helps you consider each area of your life in turn and helps assess what's off balance. It also helps you identify areas that need more attention.

Diagram.2.

The wheel-of-Life	1	2	3	4	5	6	7	8	9	10	Totals
Business/career											
Finance											
Health											
Family &Finance											
Romance											
Personal growth											
Fun & recreation											
Physical environment											
									Total		

Create a similar chart with 8 segments [see diagram.3.] and name them as I have, so that each segment is titled the same as the one above. Then place a dot representing 1 to 10 from the *"Wheel-of-Life"* in each segment, complete it by joining the dots together.

If you like you can colour in each segment and see how the dots line up; you see they don't form a perfect Pie-Chart. It's an eye-opener and very informative because you will never have everything in the segments in equal balance.

Don't despair; to obtain and to recognise that is the start of being able to begin redressing the balance by working on those areas that need attention.

Diagram.3.

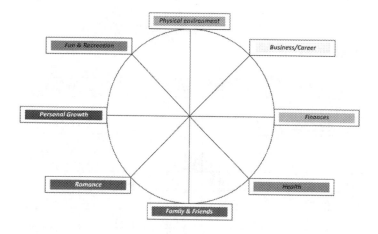

Getting your life balance correct can be a tremendous task, one that will require a lot of self-belief and confidence, which hopefully you are now enjoying. However, we also know that if you're forced to work over-night or even a few late-nights it can unbalance your health. It could also damage the relationships you have by adding extra pressure, pressure you could certainly do without because you could become very tired and impatient with you children, spouse and people around you. You're not being your normal cheerful disposition so the physical environment suffers because you haven't been paying attention to your spouse for a while. *(I know this to be the case because as mentioned earlier I was a workaholic and it did damage my marriage and relationships with my children; which by the way, I think I've been forgiven for now).*

You will always do your best to make up for the time you spent working and then spend the next day neglecting other areas to recover. Life can be a bad merry-go-round and trying to break out of it is very difficult but it's not impossible. Let me tell you; you're not alone on that wheel of life. You can, when you know where you stand, because the chart shows you the areas that you need to worked on. Now you can start addressing those individual segments.

The wheel of life exercise is used by many life coaches because it helps to give a snapshot of a person's life so far. It's also very useful in helping highlight where things might not be quite in balanced. However, do remember, though, that to increase happiness or wellbeing in a person's life, there are two possible strategies that can be adopted. You can work on the weak areas that are causing the problems but reducing unhappiness is not the same as creating more happiness, so the second strategy would be to work on areas where things are going very well and give them more time still.

Review this chapter

✓ *How much do you think you've now changed*

- *A large amount:*   *Yes-No* _____
- *A reasonable amount:*   *Yes-No* _____
- *Not a lot:*   *Yes-No* _____

✓ *Are you now working pro-actively to change? Write down what you think you're going to change:*

_____

_____

_____

_____

_____

_____

_____

_____

✓ *Explain how you feel now that you've realised that the "Fire-in-your-belly" is burning:*

_____

_____

_____

_____

_____

_____

_____

_____

✓ *Do you now think that your Life balance is in alignment? Are you now more comfortable to go forward? Write what you feel you will now do to move forward:*

_____

_____

_____

_____

_____

_____

_____

_____

✓ *Looking forward for the next 12 months, do you feel you can now add more quality to your life?*
Yes___ No___
Write down any further thoughts that you feel may help you achieve what you would like?

_____

_____

_____

_____

_____

_____

_____

_____

_____

_____

Chapter 10

Self-esteem

"This chapter will help you understand a little more regarding what self-esteem is about. Although you may feel that you have low self-esteem, feel depressed and hopeless. What you're doing is looking at life in the negative form all the time. Just remember that your self-esteem is an emotional component of your own personality it is just one factor in determining how you think, feel and behave. The level of your self-esteem is largely determined by what has happened to you in your life so far. You should also realise, everything you're trying to do seems very difficult to comprehend and is far too much trouble. The world is full of people who will ignore you and often take absolutely no notice of what you're saying or suggesting".

Unfortunately Low self-esteem is becoming very much more common in today's very busy society. For those people who feel they have low self-esteem, sometimes low self-worth is found in alcohol and drug abuse when many struggle to find their level in society and the world in general. They feel and think quite negatively about themselves and any right they have to any happiness. There are lots of people out there who feel they are incapable of making any decisions. Please rest assured; there is help available to change that negative thinking!

I can remember times in my business and home life when things have been terrible, when I've felt the world closing in on top of me and there seems to be no-end to what was happening to me and around me. There has also been at least two occasions in my life when I've been told by Doctors that I may not survive the year; *but hey*, I'm still here causing trouble! I can also remember when joining groups of people at business meetings and networking events and even parties, certainly with people I didn't really know, I was shy. *I understand for all those people who know me, you don't believe that; well it's true.*

There will also have been periods in your life that will have knocked you sideways or even knocked you back. As well as times (as there have been in my life) that your self-esteem, self-belief and confidence will have been dented and in some cases knocked, maybe very severely knocked. I've found that people who like themselves have an important and emotional part to play in their feelings and a strong belief in their own self-esteem. The more you like yourself, the more you will improve, so therefore the more you're improving, the more you'll excel in the way you're doing things. Therefore, you will start building more feelings of self-belief and confidence as they grow inside you.

American psychologist <u>Abraham Maslow</u> for example, includes self-esteem in his hierarchy of needs. In this he described two different forms of esteem; the need for respect from other and the need for self-respect; in other words inner self-esteem.

Maslow states that when the first three needs of (Physiological need—Safety needs—and the needs of love affection and belonging), are satisfied the needs for esteem will become dominant. These involve the needs for both self-esteem and for the esteem one person receives from others around them. Human beings have a requirement for a stable, firmly based, high level of self-respect and respect from other people. When these needs have been satisfied only then will a person start to feel self-confident and valuable to his fellow man around him. It is when frustration sets in that a person starts to feel inferior, weak, helpless and worthless in society.

Building your self-esteem is somewhat limited, the first step you can take towards building more self-esteem is to bring more happiness into your life this in turn will mean a better future for you and your family. When you have low self-esteem you find it impossible to be the person you really want to be and so your path to happiness is somewhat limited.

The first of Maslow's Needs are; *The Basic or Physiological Need* the need for food, water and shelter, when you have a room over your head, you are warm and can feed your family. Then this fulfils your basic-need. *Are your physiological needs fulfilled?*

The next is *The Security Need;* security is the most important of our psychological needs and at times will take precedence over the physiological need: such as emotional, financial, physical and physiological. *Are your security needs being fulfilled?*

Maslow's next level is *The Social Need;* once your *basic and security* needs are met, the social needs come into to play. People need to feel they are doing their part in something. They want and need to belong to a group and more importantly; they want to be accepted. *Are your social needs fulfilled?*

The forth level is *The Recognition Need*; it is often called the *Esteem-Need*, mainly because when people feel that they are being used or not appreciated they become resentful and feel victimised. They can have mood swings and can become very disruptive. Their need for recognition must be fulfilled. *Are your esteem needs being fulfilled?*

Maslow's fifth level is; *the Self-Actualization Need:* is psychological need of self-actualization, it is the instinctive need of a person to makes the best of their unique abilities. When people are stressed or unhappy with things around them and when they feel there is no purpose in their life, very often they feel undervalued and in a rut sometimes feeling they are engaged in doing work that is beneath them and their own capabilities. They need to find work that they will enjoy and be exciting. *Is your self-actualization needs being fulfilled or do you still feel undervalued?*

Having a very positive self-esteem helps increase your confidence so you start to respect yourself a great deal more. This is very important, it's when you start again to respect others and you also will start improving your relationships with your family and friends. You will start to notice good things about your friends and business colleagues; you will stop focusing on the things that are not very pleasant about them.

Now you'll start becoming a much happier and contented person, also people will start wanting to mix with you and to be around you again. Please don't treat this as a selfish goal because what you'll start doing is contributing more as you begin again sharing yourself with those around you; which, I'm sure you'll agree can only be a good thing.

Helping yourself or self help is about being pro active and is the best way for you to carry on developing yourself when you're trying to improve your esteem. I have spoken to many of my clients about what to do about the low self-esteem their feeling; I've have supported them when they been feeling that way. However, I've pointed out to them that it's up to them *BELIEVING* in themselves again, believe in what they're doing; believe whatever they feel they can do; then start doing it. Yes, keeping a client on the correct track and believing in themselves is what I can do for them but ultimately it is up to them to improve and develop their own self-esteem, by just believing in themselves; *remember the choice is completely theirs*.

The point I'm trying to make is that it is all up to you, it's the choice about you wanting to be happy and also being a success. If you choose to be unhappy; then that's what you've chosen to be. This is what self-help is all about. Let me point out something; if you understand that this is where you are <u>now;</u> that's good because, you've taken the first step. You know something has to change; this is what self-help is all about. One thing I try to get over to clients is that persistence at what they do is very important. Consistency over a period of time *(I suggest a minimum of 90 days for the brain to accept it as the normal)* is a battle and is rarely instantaneous; it's an uphill fight although you should be able to detect some improvement by just making a few small changes in your behaviour and thinking.

Making permanent changes by improving yourself is the goal you will have given yourself, so working at it and persisting in the efforts to build your self-esteem is one thing. However, maintaining a high level of self-esteem requires you to incorporate all the learning you've picked up and confirming them as serious habit-forming. This will be the long term goal you're striving for.

Building your self-esteem through setting goals for your future is simply done, [see chapter 6]. You do it by empowering yourself through self-discipline and to become a more pro-active and much more effective person! You should start to set realistic goals <u>now</u> and of course, for the future you're striving to achieve, although it will not guarantee you immediate results but over time it will manifest it's self into your life because, of the will you have in wanting to succeed. You're now allowing yourself to succeed by shacking off all those negative emotions that have been hanging over you for some considerable time. Your now empowering yourself to set aside those long harboured self-limiting beliefs that have, over the years blocked you from reaching out and coming out of your comfort-zone and finally achieving what you're truly after.

There are things that will help you raise your self-esteem; such as listening to your body, your mind and your heart and to what their trying to tell you. If your body tells you that you've been sitting down for far too long, stand up; take a coffee break, go for a walk, stretch your legs.

You need to start taking better care of yourself; as you've been growing up have you paid more attention looking after others and not looking after yourself and just getting along with things as they turned up. If this has been the case you need to start today and take a great deal more care of yourself. When you start working on looking after yourself, you'll find that you will start becoming alive again and feeling far better than you have for a long time.

I've listed a few tips on taking better care of youself; try and eat healthier foods and avoid junk such as "Foods containing a lot of sugar, salt or fat" a healthy daily diet usually consists of:

- Five or six servings of vegetables and fruit.
- Six servings of whole grain foods like bread, pasta, cereal and rice.
- Two servings of protein foods of; beef, chicken, fish, cheese, cottage cheese or yogurts.

If you don't at the moment you should start exercising more, moving your body will help you feel better and certainly will help improve your self-esteem. Arrange times during the day or as often as possible to take some form of exercise, preferably outdoors if you can. Walking is probably the most common, you could go for a run, take your bicycle out go for a ride, even walk up and down your stairs at home or the office block; just something to get the heart pumping a little faster. If you have a health problem that may restrict your ability to exercise, check with your doctor before beginning or changing your exercise habits. Try to do something every day that will make you feel good with yourself; take time to do things you enjoy.

Are you a very busy person? Or do you feel bad about yourself? I've found that a lot of my clients have spent very little time in the past doing things that they have enjoyed doing. Time has gone away and they've forgotten what "me-time" is! It could be playing a musical instrument, doing a craft project, flying a kite with their children or in my case "the grandchildren", or maybe fishing. Write a list of things you have enjoyed doing in the past and then start doing some of those things; perhaps just one simple action from that list every day. You should then start adding to the list anything new that you would like to do both now and in the future. You may discover new things for all the family that you all enjoy.

You should start by looking at things that you've been putting off; maybe it's time to clean out the garage this weekend; so do it. Clean the inside of your car. Wash the windows on the house something your wife has been asking you to do for months. Write that letter you've being saying you'll do for weeks. It could just be saying; stop behaving in a negative way and having bad thoughts about yourself and start doing something about it.

Try using the talents and abilities you have but perhaps haven't used for a long time. Try to complete something you really would like to do; if you are good with your hands, start making things for yourself, the family and maybe friends. If you feel inclined you may have thought of being more creative in the garden perhaps digging a pond or water feature; then do something about it. If you have some spare money you could spend some on some new clothes. Start dressing in clothes that make you feel good about yourself; check out some of the new shops in your local town. A better wardrobe could very well lift the way you feel about yourself, you will become more confident in yourself and certainly your self-esteem will soar. Give yourself rewards; treat yourself to something you may not have done for a long time, it doesn't have to cost a lot it may just be a new CD or DVD.

Spend time with people who make you feel good about yourself, try spending some *me-time* with old friends, friends who you've always got on well with; avoid time spent with the *"negaholics"* who treat you badly. Make your living space a place that reflects the person you are. Whether you live in a single room, a small apartment, or a large property, make the space as comfortable and attractive for you and your family as you can, again it may just be a coat of paint. Display items that you find attractive; display mementos of your achievements or things that remind you of special times or perhaps people in your life

Start to learn something new improve your skills start using your time wisely and start some *Continuous Personal Development* this might just be learning new things over the computer researching on the internet, taking evening classes or going to a seminar, or booking on to some webinars or tele-seminars; things that will to start to stretch your mind and remove you from the malaise and the "Comfort-zone" that you have got yourself into. Of course, you may already be doing some of these things now and there's bound to be others you will need to work on, you will find that you will continue to learn new and better ways to take care of yourself. As you start to incorporate these changes into your life, your self-esteem will continue to improve and you will start to feel more relaxed at home, in work and in new company.

You will be changing your negative thoughts regarding yourself to very pro-active and positive ones. It's so very easy to think negative thought messages about yourself. These are thought messages you've picked up as you've grown up through your youth to now. You've remembered them from very many different sources, perhaps from other children, your teachers, family members and from the media such as; television and newspapers. From the prejudice and stigma in general society once you've picked them up, you start repeating these negative thought messages over and over to yourself in your mind, especially when you're not feeling a 100% or when you're going through hard or pressing times. You've made the problem worse over the years by just thinking more negative messages and thoughts on your own. Unfortunately all these negative thought messages make you feel bad about yourself and all go to lowering your self-esteem.

A few examples of *"Negative thought messages"*; include; *"I'm an idiot, I'm a loser, I never get anything right, no one ever likes me, I'm ham-fisted in everything I do, I'm no good at this, business is no good for me"*. It's very unfortunate that most people believe these *negative thought messages* and it doesn't matter how untrue or unreal they really are. They all surface under the right set of conditions and circumstances, an example could be; when you get a wrong answer, you think *"I'm so stupid"*. They may include words like; *should have, ought, or must*. The thought messages tend to imagine the worst every-time and in everything you do and I can assure you; they are hard to stop using.

You may think these thoughts or have negative thought messages and very probably are hardly aware of them at all, you need to learn that you should pay more attention to them. People say they notice more negative thinking when they are tired, sick, or dealing with stress. As you become aware of your negative thoughts, you may notice more of them. It will certainly help to look more closely at negative thought patterns to see whether or not they are true. You may want a close friend, coach or counsellor to help you with this. When you are in a good mood and when you have a strong positive attitude about yourself, ask the following questions about each negative thought you have noticed:

You should think to yourself; is this message really true?

Message: Would a person say this to another person?
      If not, why am I saying it to myself?

Message: What do I get out of thinking this thought?
      If it makes me feel badly about myself, why not stop thinking it?

You could ask someone else, someone who knows you very well and of course a person you can trust, if you should believe a certain thought about yourself. You need now to start working on and using more positive statements by working on them in your sub-conscious and then by repeating them over and over to yourself. By doing this, what your actually doing is replacing all those negative thoughts immediately you realise your thinking about them. You can't think two thoughts at the same time, so when you're thinking positive thoughts, you can't possibly be thinking of the negative ones as well. In developing these thoughts, use positive words such as *happy, peaceful, loving, enthusiastic, and warm.*

Avoid using negative words such as *"worried, frightened, upset, tired, not, never and can't"*. Don't make a statement such as *"I am not going to worry about it"*. Instead say things such as; *I will focus on the positive.* Substitute *"it would be nice if"* for *"should"*. Always use the present tense, e.g., *"I am healthy, I am well, I am happy, I have a good job"* as if the condition already exists. Use I, me, or your own name.

The two columns below, one column negative thought the other positive thought. You should work on changing your negative thoughts to positive ones by:

Negative thoughts
I don't add up to much.

Positive thoughts:

I am a valuable person.

(N) I haven't made anything of myself.

    (P) I have achieved many things in my life.

(N) I'm always making mistakes.

    (P) I do a good job of things.

(N) I'm just a fool.

    (P) I'm a fantastic person.

(N) I don't feel I deserve a good life.

    (P) I've worked to have a happy and healthy life.

(N) I feel I am stupid.

    (P) I'm an intelligent person.

Start by replacing your negative thoughts with positive ones then repeating those positive thoughts over and over to yourself; it will certainly help you if you write them down over and over again as well as repeating those positive affirmations. Hang signs around house and in your office, place them in the car say the positive thought, and repeat the thought to yourself several times when you see it.

Deep thoughts! One of the things I teach my clients is to repeat positive thoughts over and over to themselves, I do this by suggesting they play some relaxing music, in a quiet place and then just repeat *positive thought messages* for perhaps 15 minutes when they have time; it also can double as *"me-time"* for you as well. You can do this going to sleep or when rising first thing in the morning; again waking up with positive thoughts does really set you up for the day.

Keeping away from people who are always negative is not very easy; I call them *"Negaholics"* it is always very important to keep any negative thoughts relating to yourself; you should now start flipping them over in to positive ones. It is sometimes very difficult, however by setting time aside, each and every day and being consistent and persistent all so following the techniques mentioned for should I say a period of three months the brain will start to accept it as normal and you will certainly start to notice it after about six to seven weeks. As problems start to manifest themselves again repeat them; my advice is never give-up doing them anyway. All ways remember it's all down to you! *The choice is there for the taking.*

Review this chapter

✓ *Can remember times in business or your home life when things have been terrible and you didn't really know which way to turn?*

_____

_____

_____

_____

✓ *Write a list of things you have enjoyed doing in the past, this will help jog your memory.*

_____

_____

_____

_____

✓ *Write down a few talents and abilities you have but perhaps haven't used for a long time.*

_____

_____

_____

_____

✓ *What negative thoughts you have noticed you have? Write down a few and dwell on them.*

_____

_____

_____

_____

_____

_____

✓ *Give a few examples of anyone you may know where the need of Basic or Physiological Needs are not being met.*

_____

_____

_____

_____

_____

✓ *At any time in your life, have any of the security needs, not been met by yourself, friends or colleagues?*

_____

_____

_____

_____

✓ *At any time in your life have you known that your Security Needs e.g. emotional, financial, physical or physiological have not been met?*

_____

_____

_____

_____

✓ *Have you ever felt that your Social Needs have not been met? How would you prevent this from happening to you in the future?*

_____

_____

_____

_____

✓ *Can you think about making any permanent changes that would help you improve yourself?*

_____

_____

_____

_____

Chapter 11

Positive affirmations

"This chapter will help you to start thinking differently regarding the way you look at supporting your new found knowledge and the way you feel about your own self-esteem and the confidence that is now building up inside you. Affirming what you want to do and the way you can go about empowering yourself into accepting it; by developing ways of removing negative thoughts and replacing them with very positive affirmations."

Positive affirmations are mantras that are used to impress the subconscious with thoughts that will motivate you and remind you of all the latent talents inside you and will provide the self-confidence required to accomplish those visions, dreams and goals you're after. Regularly using positive affirmations will help change your attitude, behaviour patterns and habits. People who use and utilise the power of positive affirmation have said that they lead a more peaceful, interesting and fulfilling life; they also achieve peace of mind. Positive affirmations are just key *positive thought messages* to yourself as reminders; they are used as reminders helping you to keep positive messages at the forefront of your conscious mind. It's very important to regularly think your affirmations and it's a great idea to leave them out for you to see; perhaps *stuck on the fridge, by your computer or in the bedroom.* Some will be very powerful and should be reinforced; this should be done by looking into the mirror as you're repeating them. Affirmations are very powerful in supporting your *positive-attitude* and are very effective if you're thinking of changing directions in your life as well as your perspective on life.

Obscure question! If I say to you "So how do I *not* think about the white polar bear?" All you do is to think about something else! In other words; you think what you *want* to think about, not about what you *don't* want to think about.

The thinking behind Positive Affirmations is this you're going to think in a different way; you're going to be re-programming your brain by only thinking *positive-thoughts*; over-and-over-and-over again then again-and-again and again. You're going to keep well away from all those *"Negaholic"* people and all those negative thoughts. You're going to train yourself by replacing all your *negative* thoughts with *positive* affirmations. Something you should start doing every time you have any negative thoughts that come into your head; what you're going to say replacing the negative thought will be *"I like myself or I love myself as I am"* out aloud and then repeat them as often as you think fit, I would suggest a minimum of 5 times. I understand for many of you this will feel very bizarre and strange thing to do. However, as you commence doing it, it becomes second nature to you and a normal thing to do; this is when you will begin to believe it really does work.

Affirmation lists! I've found that by making a short affirmation lists is one sure way of remembering things that are going to continue to develop and build your self-esteem and therefore increase the confidence inside you. By reading your affirmation list regularly and then rewriting it from time-to-time, you will find that it definitely makes you feel good about yourself, which obviously in its self is very rewarding for you.

Make a list of: five of your strengths, for example; persistence, courage, friendliness, creativity and helpfulness.

1. _____
2. _____
3. _____
4. _____
5. _____

Will you now list five things you admire in yourself, for example; the way you've gone through your education, the good work you're doing, the way you're looking after your family, any voluntary work you doing in the local community as well as the solid relationships you've kept with your siblings.

1. _____
   _____
   _____
2. _____
   _____
   _____

3. _____
   _____
   _____
   _____

4. _____
   _____
   _____
   _____

5. _____
   _____
   _____
   _____

You should now list your five greatest achievements for example; recovering from a serious operation, graduating with a 2/1, developing computer skills, learning to drive a car or fly a plane, representing your school in a sport.

1. _____
   _____

2. _____
   _____

3. _____
   _____

4. _____
   _____

5. _____
   _____

List five things you're able to do to make yourself laugh and smile.

1. _____
   _____
   _____

2. _____
   _____
   _____

3. _____
   _____
   _____

4. _____
   _____
   _____

5. _____
   _____
   _____

List five ways that you could support or may help someone else in their life.

1. _____
   _____
   _____

2. _____
   _____
   _____

3. _____
   _____
   _____

4. _____
   _____
   _____
5. _____
   _____
   _____

Now what I would like you to do is to think deeply and make a list of at least five things that you do that will make you feel good about yourself.

1. _____
   _____
   _____
2. _____
   _____
   _____
3. _____
   _____
   _____
4. _____
   _____
   _____
5. _____
   _____
   _____

Start reinforcing your new positive self image; give yourself 15 minutes to write everything positive and good you can think of about yourself. Include special attributes, talents, and achievements. You can use single words or sentences, whichever you prefer. You can write the same things over and over if you want to emphasise them. Don't worry about spelling or grammar. Your ideas don't have to be organised. Write down whatever comes to mind. You are the only one who will see this paper. You should NOT if possible make any negative statements or using any negative words; only positive ones. When the 15 minutes are up, read the paper over to yourself. You may feel a little down when you read it because it is a new, different and positive way of thinking about yourself; a way that contradicts some of the negative thoughts you may have had about yourself. What your actually doing is; "brainstorming your own ideas to yourself"

You will find that you're feelings of doubt about yourself will start to diminish as you read through what you've written; you should read through the paper as many times as feel you can. So have it near you and in a convenient place, your pocket, purse, wallet or the table beside your bed. Try to find time to read it over to yourself a few times every day to keep reminding yourself of how great you are! I know I've mentioned it before play some nice tranquil music in a private space and read it aloud.

When developing your positive affirmations what they really are, are positive statements that you make about yourself. They make you feel much better and very much stronger in yourself, they describe ways you would like to feel all the time; sometimes, unfortunately they don't. I've certainly found over the years that positive affirmations do work, even a simple; *I can or I will* works and works very well. An affirmation helps replace any negative thinking you have with stronger and more positive thoughts. By using the power of positive affirmations and repeating them, you can recondition the brain and ultimately change how you feel and think about any situation. The following examples are affirmations and saying them with a *definite up-beat feeling* will help you in making your own list of affirmations:

- I feel good about myself.
- I take good care of myself.
- I eat right and get plenty of exercise.
- I do things I enjoy.
- I get good health care and attend to my personal hygiene needs.
- I spend my time with people who are nice to me and make me feel good about myself.
- I am a good person.
- I deserve to be alive.
- Many people like me.

Make a list of your own affirmations. Keep this list in a handy place. Read your affirmations over and over to yourself and aloud whenever you can. Share them with others if you feel you can. Write them down from time to time. As you do this, the affirmations tend to gradually become true for you. You will gradually come to feel better and stronger in yourself.

Write a personal celebratory scrapbook; a personal scrapbook at first seems a very strange thing for me to request you to do. My reasons are very simple; your accomplishments over the years are the sum-total of your life so far. It's so very important that each of your successes that you've achieved in your life celebrates ***you*** and the wonderful person you are. Don't be self-conscious, don't be shy, this is where you bring out the positive person you want to be. Included in your scrapbook should be photographs through the ages, mementos of things you've done, things you've won and the places you've been to.

Remember there is only one you, you are unique, you are your own person, you need to remind yourself constantly that you're *umero-numero,* number-one. Look at all you've achieved and hang any photographers or objects up. You should put them up in the space wherever you do your work. Take time out to look at them whenever you need to bolster your self-esteem. Try to keep yourself inspired with daily messages. Not for just one day but continue reading positive sayings, positive affirmations and stories through the week. Find ways to be in tune with the things around you; as I mentioned earlier there are many things you can do, it could be some art project, playing music. Who knows? You could just tune in to a load of creative ideas or maybe problem-solving solutions in response to some of the questions you've been asking about yourself.

Review this chapter

✓ *How will you focus your thoughts on what to think about? Write a few notes down.*

_____

_____

_____

_____

_____

_____

_____

✓ *Focus your thoughts and therefore your affirmations on ideas that you believe in, start small and then expand.*

_____

_____

_____

_____

_____

_____

_____

✓ *Take control and start thinking about where you want to get to!*

_____

_____

_____

_____

_____

_____

_____

✓ *Try to find a tranquil place, a place you know will give you peace; list 5 places that may be good!*

_____

_____

_____

_____

_____

_____

_____

_____

Chapter 12

Assertiveness

"This chapter will show you how to build and boost your assertiveness, as well as how to progress into becoming a more successful person. Giving you an insight into communicating and by expressing both positive and negative ideas in an open and honest way, also recognising your rights whilst still respecting the rights of other people allowing you to take more responsibility for yourself and your actions without blaming or judging others. It will show you how to constructively confront and find mutual satisfaction where conflict exists."

I would think carefully and ask yourself a few questions: *Firstly; How assertive are you?*

- *Will you ask for help if you require it?*
- *How often do you volunteer your opinions when you think or feel differently from others?*
- *Do you express your anger or annoyance appropriately?*
- *Can you express yourself forcefully when asking questions, in meetings?*
- *If you're unsure or confused with things; do you speak-up and ask questions?*

- *Are you able to say "no" to people, when you don't want to do something?*
- *Do you speak in a positive and confident manner, communicating caring and strength?*
- *Do you look at people when you're talking to them?*

Building your assertiveness is not as difficult as you may think. People don't generally want to transform themselves into being assertive and becoming a more dominant person. When I've talked to clients about wanting to become more assertive, what they usually mean is:

- How do I resist the pressures and dominance of the people I'm meeting face to face on a daily basis?
- How am I able to stand up to the bullies who I meet daily, both in work and outside work?
- How will I be able to exert more control in situations that are important to me?

I've found that assertiveness or dominance for the sake of being dominant is not generally a natural behaviour in most people. People aren't naturally assertive; they tend to be passive by nature, whereas highly dominant people tend to be driven by their personality and often because of their insecurity, it's certainly not something you're trained to do.

If you're seeking to be a more assertive person it will be helpful to understand the typical personality and the motivation that excessively dominant people have, they are the cause and worry to most non-assertive people.

Over the years I've found that most excessively dominant people I've met, both in business and my private world have usually been bullies and those same people deep-down have been insecure people. I know this to be true because in my earlier years in business I was that way inclined *[and by the way I'm now in my late sixties and thank the Lord I've changed],* although I'm sure some of my children might not agree! The fact is dominant people because generally are insecure very often, don't allow others to take total responsibility. This behaviour is usually conditioned from childhood for one reason or another.

A dominant bullying behaviour is effectively reinforced by the response given by the "secure" and "non-assertive" people to bullying. Have you noticed the bullies generally always have their own way? The reason generally is because the dominant behaviour of a bully is rewarded, therefore, unfortunately the cycle goes round and so it persists. Dominant bullying people, generally from a young age become positively conditioned to a bullying behaviour pattern because they have found it works and unfortunately don't know any better; *"they have not been taught differently".*

All they are doing is feeding their own ego. Very often this is planted by insecure and very ambitious parents who are always trying to manipulate people, make decisions, build empires and collect material signs of achievement and sometimes monetary wealth. I've very often found they are trying to establish a network of *"yes-people"* around them, immune to outside influences but not always. Bullies are sometimes victims as well as aggressors. Although it's not good for anyone on the receiving end of a bully's behaviour, they do actual deserve some sympathy; *by the way, I'm not proposing here that it should be the sole or significant tactic when encountering bullying.* What I'm saying is we should try to have some alternative feeling instead of being fearful or intimidated.

When people talk about wanting to be more assertive, more in control; what they mean is; I'd like to be more able to resist the pressure and dominance of people. Importantly, the non-assertive person should understand that a true starting point to non-assertive behaviour is a sign of strength, not one of weakness and very often appropriate behaviour for most situations; please don't be fooled into thinking that you always have to be more assertive.

For people who are not naturally assertive, it's possible to achieve a suitable level of assertiveness through a few simple methods and techniques, rather than adopting a more assertive personal style (which could be counter-productive and stressful, because it wouldn't be natural). People seeking to be more assertive can dramatically increase their effective influence by using just one or two of the behaviours mentioned or when confronted by a more dominant character or influence, or prior to and when dealing with a situation in which they would like to exert more control.

Here are a few methods for developing more assertive behaviour.

You need to know all the facts relating to the situation and have the details handy, do some research and be ready to produce it, maybe give out copies if necessary. Bullies don't usually prepare their facts; they dominate through bluster, force and reputation. If you are able to produce facts and figures to support or defend your position it's very unlikely that the aggressor/bully will have anything prepared in response. When you know that a situation is going to arise over which you'd like to have some influence, prepare your facts and figures, do your research, do the sums, get the facts and figures together. Then solicit opinions and views, be able to quote sources; then you will be able to make a firm case and also dramatically improve your reputation for being someone who is organised and firm.

Anticipate other people's behaviour by preparing your own stance and responses. Role-play in your mind how things are likely to happen and prepare responses according to different scenarios that could unfold, prepare other people to support and defend you. Being well prepared always increases your self-confidence enabling you to be assertive about what's important to you. Using open questioning techniques especially well thought out and open-questions will always help you when you're trying to expose flaws in other people's arguments by asking questions as a way of gaining the upper hand. This very often takes the wind out of the other person's sails in most situations. Questions that bullies dislikes most are ones that are; *deep, constructive, incisive and probing ones,* especially when the questions expose a lack of thought, preparation, consideration and consultation on their part.

You need to condition your own reactions to other people's aggression and your reaction to dominant people particularly you do this; by having your own planned reactions mapped out in your mind. This gives you thinking time and prevents you from being bulldozed in the face of someone else's attempt to dominate you without justification. You should now try visualising yourself behaving in a more solid and firmer manner by asking firm clear and probing questions, as well as presenting well-prepared facts and evidence. Practice in your mind saying "hold on a minute or I need time to consider what you have just said." Also practice saying, I'm not sure about that, it's far too important to make such a snap decision right now without more thought; also I couldn't possibly agree to such short notice. Tell me when you really need to know and I'll get back to you. There are other ways to help resist bullying people.

You should practice and condition new reactions within yourself so that there is no fear that someone might shout at you or have a tantrum and in doing so, you are not letting others win. If you're worried about your response to being shouted at then practice being shouted at until you realise it really doesn't hurt, it just makes the person doing the shouting look daft. Try practicing with your most scary friend shouting right in your face telling you to; *"do as you are told",* over and over again. In between each time saying calmly *"You don't frighten me."* Practice it until you can control your response to being shouted at.

You need to believe your own abilities because non-assertive people have very different styles and methods compared with dominant, aggressive people as well as bullies. Non-assertive people are often extremely strong in areas of process, detail, dependability, reliability, finishing things that others have started. There also very good at checking, monitoring, communicating, interpreting and understanding and working with others. These qualities and capabilities all have the potential to disarm a bully who has no proper justification. You should find out what your own strengths are and what your style is; then use them to your advantage to defend and support your case and your position. The biggest bullies' tantrum is no match for a well controlled and organised defence.

Have a little sympathy for bullies they actually need it. You need to discover the belief that non-assertive behaviour is actually very good; it's the bullies who are the ones who have the problems. Feeling sympathy for someone who threatens you means that you're resisting succumbing to fearful or intimidated feelings. They can help to move you psychologically or at least to a position where you can see weaknesses in the bully.

I've grown up knowing that aggressors and bullies are commonly children who generally have not come from a loving family! Sometimes children live out the aspirations of their parents and in many cases the parents are still acting as children themselves. They don't know any different because they've never really grown up. They need help to find greater strength and resistance and they also need a great deal of help and support.

The point above about feeling sympathy for bullies should not be seen as approval or justification for bullying.

Rather, sympathy with care should be advocated as a more constructive, stronger, alternative feeling than being fearful or intimidated by them. People responsible for bullying are the bullies, *not the victims*. So if you are a bully; get some feedback, get some help, and start growing up.

Several tactics are explained above to help tackle bullying head-on and very often these are deemed necessary. Additionally, in most western countries and many others besides, there are now serious laws and processes to protect people from bullying and these protections should be invoked whenever bullying becomes a problem. Leaders of business, teaching establishments and professional institutions should acquaint themselves with the current legislation and certainly should be leading from the front to stamp out all bullying whether physical or psychological.

You should start reading inspirational things that reinforce your belief in your values and all the good things in your natural style and yourself. Bullying can and does scar people for life, leaving them with very low self-esteem and confidence. I teach my clients to believe in themselves, have faith in themselves and their own abilities, always repeating to themselves that whatever they ardently and vividly believe in will always come true; providing they are trying hard enough and not just treading water.

Review this chapter

✓ *How assertive do you think you are now*
- *Very assertive:*   *Yes-No* _____
- *Reasonably assertive:*   *Yes-No* _____
- *Not very assertive:*   *Yes-No* _____

✓ *Name three dominant people you've known in your life and how they affected you?*

1. _____
   _____
   _____
   _____
   _____
2. _____
   _____
   _____
   _____
   _____
3. _____
   _____
   _____
   _____
   _____

✓ *Name three insecure people you know, who don't allow others to take total responsibility?*

1. _____
   _____
2. _____
   _____
3. _____
   _____

✓ *Can you bring to mind from your childhood any bullies that had an influence on you; whether good or bad.*

1. _____
   _____
   _____
   _____

2. _____
   _____
   _____
   _____

3. _____
   _____
   _____
   _____

4. _____
   _____
   _____
   _____

Chapter 13
Self-confidence

"This chapter will help show you how to get to grips with your feelings of what self-confidence is about and give you some basic pointers on developing ways of overcoming some of the inadequacies we all have formed from time to time in our respective lives. It will give you some pointers regarding the way you look, the clothing you wear when going out to meetings, your deportment, the way you hold yourself in company and just the way you portray yourself generally"

Your self-confidence is the difference between you feeling unstoppable and you being scared out of your wits. The perception you have of yourself has a tremendous amount to play on the impact you have on others and how they perceive you; after all *"Perception is reality"*. The more self-confidence you have the more determined you are to succeed. However, you must understand that many factors that affect self-confidence are generally beyond your control but there are quite a few things you can consciously do that will help you build more self-confidence.

I have listed a few strategies to give you a sharper mental picture which will help you to accomplish your potential and giving you the determination of wanting to succeed.

Self-confidence is like dressing for the occasion. It's certainly one way that will get you noticed and get you feeling very good about yourself. Although clothes alone will not make the man or woman, your clothing and the way you look will certainly have a phenomenal affect on the way you feel about yourself. After all there is no one more conscious of your appearance than you are! I've found that when you don't look good, it changes the way you carry yourself, more importantly, it shows by the way you interact with the people around you. You of course will use this to your advantage by making sure that your personal appearance is the correct for the occasion or meeting you're attending.

Being dressed correctly doesn't mean spending lots of money buying new clothes; my late mother used to say to me *"buy quality not quantity because it lasts and if things aren't going the way you planned; your clothing will always look good"*. One of the rules I therefore follow is to spend on quality and buy half as much, rather than buying myself a load of cheap clothes. In the long run you spend a lot less because expensive quality clothes don't wear out as quickly and they generally stay in style a great deal longer than cheaper ones and your self-confidence shows for all to see.

One thing I've always been proud of has been my deportment, the way I carry myself. From a very early age probably singing in the Church choir and being constantly told; "Hold your shoulders back and keep the hymn-book straight in front of you", also the Boys Brigade emphasised it. It taught you to carry yourself in such a way that you made a statement, in other words; *the way a person carries themselves tells a story*. Good posture is very important, those people with their shoulders slumped and looking down at the floor when they're walking just display a lethargic aura and a lack of self-confidence. They don't seem to be enthusiastic about anything they do and certainly don't think themselves important at all.

At all times try walking faster, set a brisk pace. Take a look around you at the way others are walking, you'll immediately understand what I'm saying. There will be people walking at a very slow pace; some looking down at their feet, there will be others who look tired and each stride seems painful. There will be people who will be striding out with purpose and energetically displaying confidence, knowing exactly what they're doing, where they're going and having people to see, places to go and important work to accomplish. Have you noticed people with confidence *walk far more quickly than those who don't?*

It's can be difficult building self-confidence back again; I know. However, it can be done. Try practicing your posture, you'll certainly be surprised; go out now for a short walk. Stand upright, shoulders back, look straight ahead, think *I'm confident* and stride out. I guarantee within a few minutes you'll be feeling more confident. You will start feeling more alert and feel a lot more empowered. Even when you're not in a hurry, you should be able to increase your self-confidence just by putting a little more PEP into your step, this will make you look and feel more important.

What are you capable of doing yourself? A lack of self-confidence is based on the belief you have in yourself, so start writing down your personal strengths. When I ask some of my clients to do this they become shy and evasive about what they know and do. A very good way of building confidence is to listen to good motivational speeches; unfortunately opportunities of listening to great speakers are few and far between. I have listed a few names in the back of the book. I visit a few breakfast meetings, *not as many as I used to do* and I am invited to speak at a few business lunches, as well as evening events. At most of these, people have the opportunity to talk for about a minute, 30-60 seconds about themselves. In the review at the end of this chapter I will challenge you to write down some strengths about yourself and when you've written them down and you're happy with them, recite them in front of your mirror, of course smiling at yourself; sounds wacky *but hey* it works, so don't knock it till you've tried it. One thing for sure is it will certainly give you a confidence boost every time you do it.

You should also ask yourself; "Do I focus too much on what I want?" When you do the mind will create a lot of reasons why you can't have them. Unfortunately, this leads you to dwell far too much on your weaknesses. One of the best ways at overcoming this is by focusing your mind into concentrating on all the things in your past that you're been grateful for. Each day try to set aside a little "me-time" to mentally think of all your accomplishments, past successes, skills, relationships and achievements in your life that you're very pleased with. I will guarantee you'll be amazed and astounded just how much you've got going for you. Go to the review at the end of this chapter and list you triumphs and accomplishments.

Very often we are far too caught up in ourselves, in our own desires and wants, we focus far too much just looking after you, *No.1;* to looking at the needs of others around us. We should stop thinking about ourselves and start concentrating on contributing more supporting others around us. One thing it will do is to stop us concentrating on our own flaws. This will increase our self-confidence because we're contributing to others and supporting other people with maximum efficiency; knowing the more we contribute in helping others, the more we'll get back in return; often with personal success and recognition.

Unfortunately, when we're having negative feelings about ourselves, we start projecting negative feelings to other people around us; very often with disparaging words, insults and sometimes, gossiping about hear-say which is not a very nice thing to do. When you're trying to break this kind of cycle of negativity you should get into a habit of congratulating people on their achievements, remember; a little praise goes a long way. Start by making an effort to compliment people around you and then what you'll find is people will start to like you better, this in turn will help your self-confidence to grow. Try looking for what is good in other people, not the worst in them; you will find that it will indirectly bring out the best in you.

When I'm giving talks motivational or presentation talks, very often in hotels, it really amuses me as to where people decide to sit themselves down. People constantly try to sit towards the back of the room I think the reason is because they're afraid of being noticed and so, by not sitting near, or on the front row, they won't be picked out. This of course only reflects their lack of self-confidence. I would urge you to now decide to sit on the front row, this will help you get over your irrational fear and help build your self-confidence. Also, you'll now start becoming more visible to those important people you want to be introduced to, as well as being visible to the people giving the talk and those people who have organised the event.

When it comes to the *questions and answer sessions* or during group meetings there are many people who don't interact or never speak-up because they're generally afraid of feeling stupid for not understanding what the speaker has said or that the people around them will judge them. This fear is not justified generally; people are more accepting these days than we give them credit for. I've very often had delegates comes up to me after a talk and ask a certain question and I've been tempted to ask *"Why didn't you ask me that during the question and answer session"* the answer is staring me in the face; they were far too timid to ask because they lacked the confidence. Try making a big effort to speak up as often as you can in all the group meetings and during the question and answer sessions. You'll become a better public speaker, gain more confidence and become recognised as a leader by your peers.

Review this chapter

✓ *How do you feel at the moment about the way you look?*

- *Dressed for all occasions?*   *Yes* ____ *No* ____
- *Not dressed for the occasion?*   *Yes* ____ *No* ____
- *Need to change?*   *Yes* ____ *No* ____
- *Want to change?*   *Yes* ____ *No* ____

✓ *Good deportment*

- *I'm proud of my deportment and the way I carry myself.*   *Yes* ____ *No* ____
- *I could carry myself in a more confident manner.*
                                      Yes ____ *No* ____
- *Do I walk now with a spring in my step?*
                                      Yes ____ *No* ____
- *Do I need to change?*   *Yes* ____ *No* ____
- *Do I want to change?*   *Yes* ____ *No* ____

✓ *Write a sixty second presentation of your strengths and what you're capable of doing; NOW!*

_____

_____

_____

_____

_____

_____

_____

_____

_____

✓ *Take time to think through all the triumphs and accomplishments you've attained in your life.*

_____

_____

_____

_____

_____

_____

_____

_____

_____

✓ *What do you think you can contribute to others around you?*

      A lot ___ A little ___ Not sure ___

✓ *Write a few lines as to what you would do if you were able to contribute to others around you.*

_____

_____

_____

_____

_____

_____

✓ *Can you think of a few people that a little praise might help them?*

_____

_____

_____

_____

_____

✓ *Where do you sit when you go into meetings or lectures?*

• *Are you a person who sits at the rear?*

Yes ___ No ____

• *Do you routinely try to sit at the front if you can?*

Yes ___ No ____

✓ *How often do you speak up in group meetings, workshops or lectures?*

A lot ___ a little ___ not sure ____

Chapter 14

Control what you need to do

"This chapter should now give you the impetus to go out and work on what you need to do. It should help you remove those niggling addictions that you're carrying on your back, looking deeply into your self-discipline and re-igniting that fire that's deep inside you and turning it into a raging Furnace".

When you are trying to regain control, you start thinking differently, you start thinking far more confidently and some very extraordinary things start to happen; you start doing things correctly and start doing things that are very important to you first, not procrastinating and wasting time. You create different behaviour patterns; this is mainly because of the way you are behaving towards other people and you start reacting differently towards others around you.

Sometimes you feel you want to go for a walk, you know it will be good for you, you know it's very good for your health and good for your family. You also realise that afterwards you feel great and you should do it regularly every day. Unfortunately, pressures builds up and you feel lazy, very often preferring to stay in and watch television instead. You are very aware that you need to change but the problem is; you don't have the inner power, perseverance and persistence to change these habits.

I'm sure it sounds very familiar. How many times have you said; *"I wish I had more will-power and self-discipline"*. How many times have you started doing something, only to give up at the first hurdle or after a very short while? I've certainly been through it myself and I'm sure you must have had similar experiences as well. All of us possess some form of addiction or habit we wished we could overcome; the habits might be smoking, laziness, eating too much, procrastination or even lack of assertiveness.

Trying to overcome habits or addictions is not easy, it requires lots of will power; you have to start believing in yourself all over again. This will not be easy, self-discipline needs courage, tenacity, self-control, and the determination to *"Succeed"*. It means digging down into your inner-strength with a determination and decisiveness that will only come when you start becoming pro-active, when you want and need to re-ignite that *"fire in your belly"* again.

What is *Will power?* It is the ability to overcome that laziness and procrastination we've mentioned several times in the book before. It's the ability to take hold of a situation, by taking control or by rejecting an unnecessary or maybe a possible harmful course of action. It's also the ability to arrive at a decision; then follow it through with dogged determination and perseverance until arriving at a *"Successful conclusion"*. It's the power from within all of us that overcomes the desire to indulge in unnecessary and useless habits. It's the inner strength that's lying dormant, or near dormant, that we all have. It is the will to overcome the mental resistance that determines us to take action. It's when we say things like; *"I can do this"*, *"I will do this"*, *"I can succeed"*, *"I will succeed"*, *"I'll show them"*, *"I know it's the correct way, so I'll do it that way"*. It is totally down to our choice again and only our choice.

We should also look at self-discipline as being the partner of will power. It gives us the stamina to continue and persevere in whatever we do. It provides us with the ability to withstand hardships and difficulties, whether they are physical, mental or emotional. It also gives us the ability of rejecting immediate satisfaction just to gain something now, rather than putting a great deal more effort and time into doing a really good quality job and having it done on time. Self-discipline should be considered as a type of selective training; it's creating new habits, thoughts, action and of course discipline which naturally helps towards improving you. It will also help reach those visions and dreams that you're after and to achieve those goals you're stretching to reach.

Self-discipline, as pointed out earlier, can be task oriented and is very selective, it is one of the last steps that you take when bringing together all that you have learned and more importantly have been putting into practice while you've been reading this book and writing in the review sections. You should now view self-discipline as a *very positive effort*, rather than one of denial. This will be a trait that, for most of us, will need to be developed. It is something we all need because it is a vital characteristic of entrepreneurial and successful people. *Why?* Nothing appears as easy as it seems, there are always unforeseen problems and challenges in the direction and paths we have chosen, as well as the visions, dreams and goals we have been planning to achieve.

I've found that you need to have both self-discipline and will-power in order to rule your positive thought patterns and to be able to be in charge of yourself. The stronger they are the more control you will have over all your thoughts and therefore subsequently, your powers of concentration will start manifesting themselves and so they will build and get stronger.

When you're the master of your inner self, you will start to enjoy inner peace and therefore happiness, outside events won't sway your decisions and circumstances will have no power over your peace of mind. This might sound too unreal for you but experience will prove to you that all the above are true and that by believing that it will be, you will achieve! These abilities are essential for your self-growth, they give you control over your daily life, they help you improve your habits and behaviour and they are one of the *"tools in your tool-box"* for you to attain *"Success"*.

To keep on overcoming setbacks we must persevere and be very strong. One of my recent *"Thought for the Day"* stated it quite well; *"Set your goals high, and don't stop trying till you get there."* If you have any sort of problem, you must persevere and be strong. Unfortunately, excessive bad habits of any kind will foster very low-esteem and therefore will result in a lack of confidence. If you do suffer from any obsessions and find difficulty in controlling yourself you may blame or punish yourself. The reverse can also be true, low self-esteem will cause some of the problems; this of course is the vicious circle.

This is where self-discipline helps you to control your actions and will help you to stay on track. If you do suffer any of the above, you need to break away and start to cure yourself. You should make use of helpful friends and colleagues, or you may seek the help of a professional coach or mentor. *All you are asking for is someone to listen to you and support you in your efforts.* I have many business colleagues I can call on, bounce ideas off and of course, I have many supportive friends in my Church community. I can draw comfort from them; I especially did when I had my heart attack and By-Pass operation in 2004 and again when in 2007 I was diagnosed with Leukaemia, then also in 2009 when diagnosed with Type 2 Diabetes.

Many people say to me; "Why do you write a daily blog?" "Why do you coach and mentor people?" "Why do you write articles, e-books and books, when you have so many things wrong with you?"

My answer to all those above is very simple; I started doing all those things for ME to help ME fight what was wrong inside ME. Now what has happened, other people are drawing on MY strength and my writings, this gives me more fight to carry on doing what I'm doing. I know that there are many people trying to go it alone out there and I know that is so very difficult.

Have faith in YOURSELF; faith that you will reach whatever you are seeking. When you truly believe in YOU, you are able to trust in yourself and have sufficient desire and self-discipline; take it from me life comes and becomes, very easy.

Chapter 15

What next?

This is now up to you; you have read the book and I do hope it has given you some solid ideas of where you would like to go from here. Without a benchmark for people to work to and indeed to strive to reach, you could still be floundering in the dark!

So, in *chapter one, The Great Mystery;* I tried to say to you that your *"Success"* will only come from what is inside you, from your visions and dreams; your success comes from within, that burning fire in your belly. Therefore, trying to identify this, from today forward and saying to yourself that the future you want and desire, for you and your family is here to grasp. However, it is for you to make that choice; *"that is your choice and your choice alone".* There are hundreds of thousands; probably hundreds of millions of people who do not have any choice of their own at all; you do *"make the best of it!"*

Chapter two was about Self-belief; we looked at creating more self-belief in your life and the need to change your way of thinking and perhaps the need to change what you are doing NOW! I realise that sometimes It's very difficult to admit things aren't the way you had hoped they would be and certainly after someone has said something you don't agree with, you feel like saying; *"they don't have the right to tell me that"*. You now need to start believing that you're the equal to anyone but please don't look down or be patronising; just treat people the way you yourself would like to be treated. Just remember your success is built on your assets so you must use those assets to the full. Use your assets wisely, each and every day, in your life, you've made decisions because *"the choice was yours"*. So believe in yourself!

Chapter three, You're never too late to Learn we looked at the importance of continuous personal development and what can be done after having gone through any sort of set-back and to get back in touch with your own values. Also, to start setting meaningful goals again, you need to start recapping and identifying those misplaced *"visions and dreams"*; that you have had. What the chapter is saying is never give up, never stop learning, never stop striving to reach the top; remember the person who thinks they can, will, but the person who thinks they can't, will not.

Chapter four, Your core-values we looked at the values you hold dear, by getting you to go back to square one. This could be your family, maybe your business, the freedom you have or the environment. It may have been the mentors and peers you looked up to and the culture that you've been brought up in. They have all moulded the personal values that you believe in. The chapter tries to help you identify and establish your own core values helping you to become a more resilient and pro-active person.

Chapter five, What motivates you gave you support and guidance into using your positive thoughts over the negative ones that are forever manifesting. Motivation is after all only a word; although the meaning to most people signals the desire to win. The desires to learn and succeed are equally important. The chapter has shown you where your motivation comes from, it's the fire in your belly that builds up to a mighty furnace and it's in the sayings; I can, I will, I shall. It comes from within because this kind of motivation is solely driven and fired by YOU, through your "self-belief". However, if you haven't got motivation deep within you, you certainly won't get very far.

Chapter six, Realistic goal setting will have helped you break maybe one or two bad habits or maybe just help you to restructure your life a little bit. It should have shown you the importance of personal goal setting as being the most effective way of helping you define and achieve your visions and dreams. After all, setting your goals is one of the main tools you have in your tool-box and should be re-visited and up-dated frequently. I've shown you the most effective way of putting together your intentions setting your goals by using the SMART goal approach. Doing a SMART analysis will ensure that your goals contain all the most important points that help you to maximise the goal setting process.

Chapter seven, Take positive action will have brought out in you the desire to act positively with your visions and dreams. It will have brought to the forefront that waiting around being re-active is certainly not the way to get ahead in life. Entrepreneurs and winners aren't people who've waited for chances to come their way. They're the people that have pro-actively gone out of their way to forge themselves forward. In the chapter I've mentioned Duncan Bannatyne's book *"Anyone can do it"*. It would be remiss of me not to mention a couple of other people; Theo Paphitis book *"Enter the dragon"* and Alan Sugar's autobiography *"What you see is what you get"*. These three people have all come up through the school of hard-knocks and won through by sheer determination and having a emphatic desire to win and never give up. I have mentioned at the back of the a few more people it would be an idea to look at.

Chapter eight, Managing your time I feel this chapter will have made you realise that the range of skills inside your head that you haven't been using, has been because you've been working on other things and not thinking outside the box. You now have more ideas on how to manage your time more efficiently on allocating your time and delegating tasks including projects and analysing the time spent on planning.

Chapter nine, Change I'm sure this chapter has demonstrated that you must embrace and encourage change in your life if you really want to succeed. Having more self-belief, confidence and motivation, you need to say, *OK, so I'm here now, where do I go from here?* Work out what you need to change and what you need to do. You need to be hard with yourself and extremely pro-active, start changing your attitude and mindset and think of using a more positive vocabulary. Stay well away from all the "Negaholics". Surround yourself with positive people, people who have direct action written on their foreheads.

Chapter ten, Self-esteem will have given you some understand regarding what self-esteem is about. You may still feel that your self-esteem is not where you would like it to be. You could feel at times a little depressed and maybe hopeless but hey, looking at life in the negative form as you used to; is now being replaced and you are now mixing with pro-active and positive people.

The level of your self-esteem you now realise and everything you're doing, is not as difficult to comprehend as it was. Before you found it far too much trouble and you are finding it now so much easier. You're now looking at the world full of people who are not completely ignoring you and are now taking notice of what you're saying or what you're suggesting.

Chapter eleven, Positive affirmations was about starting to think differently, looking at supporting your new found knowledge and the way you felt about your self-esteem. You are now affirming to the world that you are empowering yourself into accepting challenges and planning by removing all those negative thoughts that have been building up by replacing them with positive affirmations, mental pictures of you. You are now reaching successful conclusions by acting pro-actively in all the things your now doing.

Chapter 12, Assertiveness this chapter will have shown you how to build and boost your assertiveness and the need to believe your own abilities. Helping develop you into being a more successful person. Giving you an insight into communicating with others by expressing your positive as well as negative ideas in an open and honest way. Recognising your rights whilst still respecting the rights of other people and taking responsibility for yourself and actions without blaming or judging others. It will have shown you how to constructively confront and find mutual satisfaction where conflict exists.

Chapter 13, Self-confidence this chapter will have shown you the reasons why it's so important to get to grips with your feelings, giving some basic pointers on ways of overcoming your inadequacies that have formed over time. It has given you some ideas in your dress sense, the clothing to wear, your deportment, how to hold yourself in company and the way you portray yourself generally. Your self-confidence displays the important and different feelings you have of being unstoppable. It will have give you a perception about yourself along with a tremendous amount to play on regarding the impact you now have on others and how those same people now perceive you; after all *"Perception is reality"*. It will have shown you that the more self-confidence you have, means the more determined you will be to succeed. Although, it must be understood that many factors affecting self-confidence are generally beyond your control there are quite a few things you can consciously do that will help you build more self-confidence.

Chapter 14, Control is about your own ability to now move forward with a plan of action on where you want to go. It told you about those niggling addictions that you're carrying on your back and suggested that you look deeply at your self-discipline. More importantly it guided you into how to re-ignite that fire deep inside you and turned it into a raging furnace. I do hope this chapter and indeed the book will have given you the impetus to go out and work on what you need to do. You will have gained confidence in yourself and what you do! It now has given you commitment to go out to do it. However, the culmination will be for you to now walk forward with your head high, your back ramrod straight, with a pro-active attitude toward life and helping people get what they want.

Notes

Chapter 1

Obituary of Gerry White <u>Sep 3 2008</u> Liverpool Echo
Give the child Francis Xavier quote

Chapter 3

Nicholson McBride (www.nicholsonmcbride.com)
Nicholson McBride "Resilience Questionnaire (<u>www.testyourrq.com</u>)
Vincent T Lombardi (<u>www.saidwhat.co.uk/quotes/favourite/vincent t lombardi</u>)

Chapter 4

(Senator John Kerry (American Senator 1943)

Chapter 5

Jim Rohn Library website (www.achievementlibrary.com/jim-rohn.htm)
Zig Ziglar official website (<u>www.ziglar.com</u>)
Dr Heinz Weihrich Professor of Global Management and Behavioral Science | School of Business and Management | University of San Francisco (usf.usfca.edu/fac_staff/weihrichh/home.htm)
Aristotle (<u>384-322 BCE</u>) http://www.philosophypages.com/ph/aris.htm

Chapter 8

Mary Engelbreit: If you don't like something change it; if you can't change it, change the way you think about it.

Chapter 13

Motivation speakers; Jim Rohn, Bob Proctor, Zig Ziglar

Motivational speakers and people to take note of:

Anthony Robbins also known as Tony Robbins, suffered many hardships in life when his mother divorced and remarried twice. He took on the last name of his second father. Later in life he was diagnosed with a tumour of the brain, thus resulting in abnormal growth spurts and his large hands and feet. His bestselling books like 'Awaken the Giant Within' are a tribute to this legend.

Baroness Grey-Thompson DBE Is a multi-gold winning paralympiam and one of the United Kingdom's most respected sportswomen as well as a popular inspirational Speaker.

Chris Bonington Is one of the United Kingdom's greatest explores. Chris has climbed all the major mountains in the world and is an inspiration.

Colonel Bob Stewart An army officer for 26 six years, he is best known for his command of the United Nations peacekeeping forces in Bosnia. He was awarded the Distinguished Service Order for leadership and gallantry. He is now a broadcaster and regularly on all main television channels.

David Bellamy OBE Is a British botanist, author, broadcaster and environmental campaigner. He is a denier of anthropogenic global warming and a very enigmatic after dinner Speaker. He has written many papers on the conservation of the planet and he has written at the very least 45 books as well as numerous films and documentaries on the environment

Duncan Bannatyne OBE Is a Scottish serial entrepreneur, philanthropist and author. His business interests include hotels, health clubs, spas, media, TV, stage schools, property and transport. He is most famous for his appearance as a a long standing Dragon on BBC's Dragons Den. He was appointed as an OBE for his contribution to charity.

Jacqueline Gold Chief Executive of Gold Group International which includes Ann Summers & Knickerbox, she is an inspiration to thousands of women and does numerous charity fundraising.

James Caan is a UK entrepreneur from Pakistan. Caan has been building and selling businesses since 1985, including Alexander Mann Group, Humana International, and the private equity firm Hamilton Bradshaw. a company with a turnover of £130m and operations in 50 countries and then sold the company in 2002. He is better known for his long standing position on BBC's Dragons Den. He is also known through The James Caan Foundation, it supports a number of philanthropic projects with organisations including Princes Trust, Marie Curie, Children in Need, Comic Relief, Islamic relief, vinspired, Care foundation, NSPCC and Mosaic.

John McCarthy John was working in Beirut for a television news agency when the political situation escalated and it became very dangerous to stay. Unfortunately John was taken hostage in April 1986 and held for five years. He was appointed a Commander of the Order of the British Empire in 1992. John is also an Author having written four books.

Karren Brady Is known as the first woman in football and she has been Managing Director of Birmingham City Football Club since 1993 turning the clubs fortunes around. Karren is also on The Apprentice with Lord Sugar). She has also published four books including two novels.

Lawrence Dallaglio OBE (Was the former England Rugby Captain, Captain of Wasps before retiring, he is now a very entertaining motivational speaker as well as a keynote speaker.)

Major Ken Hames (Rtd) Served in the British Forces for 25 years and is one of the elite British Officers to have worn the red beret of the Parachute Brigade, the green beret of the Royal Marines and the sand beret the Special Air Services). He is a motivational Speaker and specialist television presenter.

Lord Alan Sugar Is the founder of the electronics company Amstrad. He was chairman of Tottenham Hotspur from 1991 to 2001, he rocketed to celebrity status in his hit TV show "The Apprentice" which has been broadcast annually from 2005. He has written a book called "What you see is what you get" and is well worth reading.

Michelle Mone OBE She left school aged 15 with no qualifications and is the founder and co-owner of MJM International and creator of Ultimo, the UK's leading designer lingerie brand. Listed as one of the top three female entrepreneurs in the UK and recently voted as the number one woman in business by Glamour Magazine, Michelle has built a hugely successful career on an incredibly simple concept: giving today's women what they want.

Peter Jones CBE As a schoolboy, Peter dreamt of running a multi-million pound company. He reached that dream with interests mobile phones, television, media, leisure and property. Peter became a television celebrity on the show Dragons' Den. His book "Tycoon" written in 2007 gives a good account of his life.

Richard Denny Over the past 20 years he has become a legend *as a business growth specialist and an inspirational business speaker. He is probably unique in that his presentations not only motivate, inspire and educate his audience. Richard has written over five books on selling.*

Robert Craven Spent 5 years running training and consulting at Warwick Business School and set up his own consultancy in 1988. Sought after speaker on entrepreneurship. He has written four books and they are worth reading, they are thought provoking.

Ruth Badger Is from Wolverhampton who left school at 16, having had various part time jobs. Ruth became a Senior Management Executive before at the age of 27 she entered the television show "The Apprentice" and is best known as the 2006 runner-up. Since then she **established in January 2006 The Ruth Badger Consultancy Limited and is** also a popular after dinner speaker.

Sir Clive Woodward OBE As the architect of Britain's greatest rugby achievement, he has secured his place in history. His reputation as a world-class leader makes him one of the most sought after public speakers industry-wide. He is currently director of Elite Performance at the British Olympic Association working towards success for the London 2012 Olympics. He has written three books, yes they are all about winning.

Simon Weston **OBE** In 1982 the Sir Galahad was destroyed in Bluff Cove on the Falkland Islands. On board was Simon Weston, Welsh Guardsman, a name and face that was going to become well known for his struggle to overcome his injuries (46% burns) and redefine his role in life. Simon's message is one of achievement, of triumph over adversity, of seizing the moment and succeeding. Simon has written 3 autobiography's the in 2004 Moving On.

Sir Richard **Branson** Has achieved what most young professionals could only dream of: incredible wealth, fame, and acknowledgment, all the while still managing to have a good time. Sir Richard is a flamboyant British billionaire that has built his company (Virgin) into one of the world's biggest brands. He written many books on his life and also about business and getting started.

Theo Paphitis Is a British entrepreneur of Greek Cypriot origin. He started his career at the age of 16 as a tea boy/

filing clerk with Lloyds of London insurance brokers before making his first foray into retail at the age of 18. At the age of 20 he moved into finance—property and corporate, specialising in turnarounds, setting up his own company at the age of 23. He is best known for his appearances on the television show Dragon Den and as former chairman of Millwall football club.

Zig Ziglar, Hilary Hinton is one of the most successful motivational speakers in America. When at a tender age, his father, a successful businessman, passed away, Ziglar was in terms "a reborn Christian". An ardent football fan, he also teaches students in a Baptist Church apart from his main business of being one of the most successful motivational speakers of America. He has written a large number of books and has many CD's and DVD's to his credit.